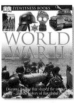

Eyewitness
MONEY

Ancient Italian bronze coin of the city of Hatra, 3rd century B.C.

Australian cupro-nickel 50 cents, 1970

Bolivian gold 8-scudos coin, 1841

Indian gold "pagodas," 17th–19th century

Indian gold mohur, 17th century

Ceylon (Sri Lanka) 10-cent note, 1942

Ancient Roman medals showing minting (below) and banking (right).

Djibouti French colonial note, 20th century

Ancient Greek silver coin showing Alexander the Great, 4th century B.C.

Moroccan bronze coins, unseparated, as taken from the mould, 19th century

Spanish silver "piece of eight" reales from Mexico, 1732

Gold 10-ducat coin of Transylvania, 17th century

Eyewitness
MONEY

Written by
JOE CRIBB

USSR cupro-nickel
ruble, 1967

Ancient Chinese
bronze hoe-
shaped coin,
6th century B.C.

American gold
"eagle," 1797

Siamese paper money,
1860s

Japanese
Temple note,
19th century

Octava pars
ticalis
One eighth
of tical

English brass halfpenny
token, 1665

Zambian
bronze penny, 1966

DK Publishing, Inc.

English gold soverign (1901) and brass sovereign balance

LONDON, NEW YORK, MUNICH,
MELBOURNE, and DELHI

Project editor Linda Martin
Art editor Richard Czapnik
Senior editor Sophie Mitchell
Senior art editor Julia Harris
Editorial director Sue Unstead
Art director Anne-Marie Bulat
Special photography Chas Howson,
Department of Coins and Medals, the British Museum

REVISED EDITION
Editors Barbara Berger, Laura Buller
Editorial assistant John Searcy
Publishing director Beth Sutinis
Senior designer Tai Blanche
Designers Jessica Lasher, Diana Catherines
Photo research Chrissy McIntyre
Art director Dirk Kaufman
DTP designer Milos Orlovic
Production Ivor Parker

This Eyewitness ® Guide has been conceived by
Dorling Kindersley Limited and Editions Gallimard

This edition published in the United States in 2005
by DK Publishing, Inc.
375 Hudson Street, New York, NY 10014

05 06 07 08 09 10 9 8 7 6 5 4 3 2 1

A catalog record for this book is
available from the Library of Congress.

ISBN 0-7566-1389-2 (Hardcover) 0-7566-1398-1 (Library Binding)

Color reproduction by Colourscan, Singapore
Printed in China by Toppan Printing Co.,
(Shenzhen) Ltd.

Discover more at
www.dk.com

Ancient Roman
silver coin,
3rd century B. C.

Ancient Indian
gold coin,
1st century A. D.

Australian
aluminum-brass
two-dollar
coin, 1998

Ottoman Turkish
gold zeri-mahbub
18th century

Ancient Roman
gold bar made from
melted-down coins, 4th century

Tonga cupro-nickel
one-pa´anga coin, 1977

Ancient Greek silver:
broken coin, cut ingot, and
wire from Taranto (Italy) hoard

Ancient Chinese bronze
knife-shaped coin, 3rd
century B.C.

Persian
silver wire
"lairn" coin,
16th century

Contents

Indian cupro-nickel
10-paise coin, 1964

Chinese silver good-luck coin
charm, 19th century

This is money

It is difficult to imagine a world without money; every country has its own, and its history reaches back to the earliest written records of human activity. But what is this thing called money? Money can be many different things: For most people, it is coins, banknotes (bills), plastic cards, and money in the bank. But for some people in the not-too-distant past, it has been feathers, stones, beads, and shells (pp. 8–9), for these were the objects they considered valuable. What allows us to describe all of these things with the same word, "money," is that they are all an acceptable and recognized means of payment. This even applies to the money you cannot see or feel – the money that is stored in bank computer records, and which can be spent in the same way as the coins and notes in your pocket.

EVERYDAY MONEY
Banknotes, coins, and plastic cards come in various shapes, sizes, and colors, but they all share the same name, "money," because they are all used to make payments.

The earliest money

It is not known exactly when money was first used. The oldest written records of it are from Ancient Mesopotamia (now in southern Iraq) about 4,500 years ago. Ancient Mesopotamian cuneiform (wedge-shaped writing) inscriptions describe payments being made with weighed amounts of silver. Since then, weighed amounts of metal have been used as money in many parts of the world, and this practice led to the invention of coins (pp. 10–11).

GOOSE WEIGHT
So that silver and other goods could be weighed accurately, the Ancient Mesopotamians had officially made weights. This example weighs about 30 shekels. There were 60 shekels in a mina.

MESOPOTAMIAN MONEY
The inscription on this tablet commemorates "prices" during the reign of Sin-Kasid of Uruk (B.C. 1865–1804): "In the course of his reign, one shekel [a unit of weight] of silver on the local standard could buy three measures of barley, twelve mina of wool, ten mina of bronze, or three measures of sesame oil, according to the price in his kingdom."

HAMMURABI'S LAWS
This big stone column shows a god giving Hammurabi, King of Babylonia (B.C. 1792–1750) laws referring to how silver should be used. Law 204 says: "If a common man slaps the face of another common man, he must pay ten shekels of silver as compensation."

Ten

Twelve

Wool

Barley

Bronze

CUNEIFORM
The decipherment of cuneiform script has enabled us to discover many other descriptions of money paid in the form of weighed amounts of silver in ancient Mesopotamia. The characters above appear in the inscription on the tablet.

Lump of gold

EGYPTIAN WALL-PAINTING
This ancient Egyptian wall-painting (14th century B.C.), found in a tomb at Thebes, shows gold rings being weighed on a balance. The Egyptians used balances and weights to measure the value of precious metals.

EGYPTIAN HOARD
The ancient Egyptians also developed a system for making payments with weighed amounts of metal; records exist of gold, silver, and copper being weighed out as payments. Because the weight set its value, the shape and size of the metal was unimportant. The money was as varied in shape as the bars, rings, and lumps of silver in this 14th-century-B.C. hoard from el-Amarna.

Heavy silver bar

STONE WEIGHT
The hieroglyphic inscription on this small Egyptian stone weight is faint, but it tells us that the weight was used for weighing gold. A clearer version of the hieroglyph for "gold" can be seen on an Egyptian gold coin (p. 57).

Silver in this form was very convenient since it was easy to cut into smaller pieces

Position of string on the scale showed how much the silver in the pan weighed

Ivory rod marked with scale

IN THE BALANCE
Although the Chinese had coins from the 6th century B.C. (p. 11), they did not make gold and silver into coins, but weighed it out for payment – right up to the 1930s. Official weights were made, but for everyday business, traders used small hand-balances like this one. The silver ingots were made in special shapes to show where they came from. The ingots below are all from northeast China, and were made in the 19th century.

Brass counterweight was moved along the scale until the ivory rod hung level

Burmese weight made of bronze

The largest ingot weighs one liang (ounce), and the smallest one weighs one-tenth of one liang. Ingots as heavy as 50 liang were also used

Flower pattern

"FLOWER SILVER"
The only official money in 18th-century Burma was weighed amounts of silver. Most of the silver was poured out into pancake-shaped discs known as "flower silver." The name refers to the patterns on the silver, which were made by blowing through a pipe at the metal as it set.

LION WEIGHT
All the official Burmese weights were in the form of animals such as elephants, ducks, bulls, and lions (like this one). A star-shaped mark was stamped on the base of each weight to show that it had been checked by the King's official.

Funny money?

As heavy as stone, as light as a feather, "money" comes in many forms. The objects on these pages may seem very curious, but they were not strange to the people who used them. In some tribal societies, payments were made with objects that had a recognized value: ornaments like shells; tools like hoes; foodstuffs like salt and grain; and cloth (pp. 56–57), all of which were counted out in payments. As with our money today, and the weighed metal money of Ancient Mesopotamia (p. 6), tribal societies had very strict rules about the value and payment of their money; it was generally used to settle social obligations, like marriage payments, compensation, and fines.

MEXICAN MONEY AX
When the Spanish conquistadors entered Mexico (p. 39), the Mexicans were using cacao (chocolate) beans and small copper axes in payments. The money axes were too fragile to be used as tools!

SUDANESE MONEY HOE
There are many reports from 19th-century Africa of iron hoes being used to make payments in wedding settlements. The Ancient Chinese also made payments with hoes.

STONE MONEY
The stone below is a small example of the stone discs used to make social payments and settle disputes by the people of Yap, an island in the Pacific Ocean. The largest examples measured up to 12 ft (4 m) across!

Stone is made of aragonite, a form of limestone

Reed binding to prevent breakage

Herd of African cattle

ETHIOPIAN SALT BAR
Bars of rock salt were widely used both for cooking and as money in Ethiopia until the 1920s. The bars were bound in reeds to prevent breakage. Elsewhere in eastern Africa, herds of cattle are still considered symbols of wealth and status.

MONEY COWRIE SHELLS

The earliest reports of payments with cowrie shells were from China about 3,500 years ago. When the Chinese writing system was being developed, the cowrie shell was thought the best symbol for money (right). Cowrie shells were also used in 10th to 8th-century India, 7th-century Thailand, and 9th-century Africa.

Treasure

To sell

To buy

To barter

Cowrie shell symbol

NIGERIAN COPPER MANILLA

Copper rings, known as manillas, were used from the 15th century in West Africa to make payments. They were still being used until 1948 (p. 56) among the Ibo people of eastern Nigeria.

Cowrie-shell decoration

Beads made from clam shells

FEATHER MONEY

This "money" was made from tiny red feathers glued together and tied onto vegetable-fiber coils that could be up to 30 ft (10 m) long. They were used by the Pacific islanders of Santa Cruz as payments at marriage ceremonies, and to acquire ocean-going canoes. The brighter the feathers were, the more valuable the coil.

Square design may represent a Native American village

WAMPUM

This belt of beads (wampum) was made from white and purple clam shells by Native Americans in North America. Early European settlers told how the local people used the beads as money, usually to settle agreements between villages. Wampum belts often had designs worked into them; each of the three "squares" on this belt may have represented a different village.

Salt bar

The first coins

COINING TOOLS
Roman coin showing ancient tools for making coins: punch (top), anvil (center), hammer (right), and tongs (left).

COINS ARE PIECES OF METAL marked with a design that instantly shows that they are money. The earliest-known coins were made during the 7th century B.C. in the kingdom of Lydia (in the country we now call Turkey). Weighed lumps of electrum (a mixture of gold and silver) were used by the Lydians as money, and were stamped with pictures to confirm their weight and therefore their value in payments. This process of stamping is called "minting." The shape of the coins was unimportant. The stamp on the coin was a personal seal or "badge" that identified the person who had guaranteed the coin's weight; the Lydian kings used a lion's head on their coins. This new method of organizing money was a great success and soon spread into Europe. Although the Lydian invention was the first, the same idea was developed elsewhere to standardize other forms of metal money: copper lumps in southern Russia and Italy, bronze tools and shells in China, silver rings in Thailand, and gold and silver bars in Japan.

Mark made by punches

One-stater coins

1/6-stater coins

1/24-stater coin

LYDIAN ELECTRUM COINS
The weight of Lydian money was measured in units called "staters," about 1/2 oz (14 g) each. Fractional coins were also made; coins as small as 1/96 stater were made! Each metal lump was placed on an anvil, and the punches were pushed into the lump with a hammer. Because the anvil had been engraved with the lion's head emblem of the Lydian kings, these coins (B.C. 600) now had this image stamped on them.

Greek letters

Marked ingot made of copper

PERSONAL SEALS
The Greek letters on the coin from western Turkey (left) mean "I am the seal of Phanes." The design is similar to the Greek seal (above), which names its owner, Mandronax.

Caria, c. B.C. 530

Andros, c. B.C. 525

Ceos, c. B.C. 525

Aegina, c. B.C. 540

Athens, c. B.C. 540

EARLY SILVER COINS
The idea of coinage spread from western Turkey into the Greek world. Within 100 years, coins were issued as far away as Italy and Libya. The pictures on four of these coins were the emblems of the place of issue: a lion for Caria in Turkey; a vase, a squid, and a turtle for the Aegean islands of Andros, Ceos, and Aegina. The beetle is the emblem of an Athenian official. These coins can be dated because they were buried as an offering to the goddess Artemis (right) in the foundations of her temple at Ephesus, built around B.C. 560.

Knife-shaped coin

Olbian dolphin coins, 4th century B.C.

Olbian round coin, 4th century B.C.

Hoe-shaped coin

CAST COPPER COINS

Before coinage was adopted in Olbia in Russia, and in Rome and other Latin and Etruscan (pre-Roman) cities of Central Italy, weighed pieces of cast copper were used as money. Under the influence of Greek coins, designs were added to these copper ingots (pieces of cast metal made in a mold) to turn them into coins. In Olbia, most of the cast copper pieces were round, but some were cast in the shape of a dolphin, probably because Olbia was on the Black Sea coast.

Cowrie-shell shaped coin

CHINESE TOOL AND SHELL COINS

The earliest Chinese coins (about B.C. 500) were made from bronze in the shape of the tools and cowrie shells that had previously been used as money by the Chinese. The tool-shaped coins were too fragile to be used as actual tools!

ELEPHANT-SIZED COIN!

In Rome, the earliest marked ingots kept the rectangular shape used earlier for unmarked ingots. The Indian elephant shown here is a reference to the war elephants of a Greek army that invaded southern Italy in B.C. 280.

JAPANESE SHOGUN

Shoguns were fearsome military dictators who ruled Japan from the 12th to the 19th century.

THAI RING-COINS

Before they made coins, the people of Thailand used weighed silver rings as money. When the rings were made into coins (17th century), their shape was changed by bending or hammering. They were then stamped with official marks.

Gold coin, 1601

JAPANESE INGOT COINS

During the late 16th and early 17th centuries, the Japanese leader Ieyasu, who later became the first Tokugawa Shogun, reorganized Japan's monetary system (p. 54). His gold and silver coins were in the form of hammered or cast slabs, like the ingots previously used as money.

Silver coin, 1601

Gold coin, 1818

The first paper money

Banknotes are only pieces of paper, yet they are accepted as money because it is what they represent that is valuable. It was the Chinese who first saw the advantages of handling money in the form of printed paper documents. During the 10th century, the Chinese government issued heavy iron coins that were worth little. People started to leave their coins with merchants and to use the handwritten receipts the merchants gave them instead. In the early 11th century, the government took over from the merchants and printed receipts that could be used officially as money, and, to make the system simpler, the receipts were given fixed values.

DIFFICULT TO LOSE!
The banknote below was quite large to carry around. The largest note ever issued, it measured 9 x 13 in (22.8 x 33 cm).

JAPANESE NOTE
The idea of paper money spread to Japan during the 17th century. Most Japanese notes were issued by feudal clans and temples.

Japanese "bookmark" note of 1746

TEMPLE MONEY
Japanese temples – like this one in Kyoto – acted like banks, issuing their own paper money.

CHINESE PAPER MONEY
In the center of the design of this 14th-century Chinese note, you can just see the 1,000 coins it represented. The coins would have weighed about 8 lb (3.5 kg). Perhaps it is not surprising that the Chinese were the first to use paper money!

ENGLISH MONEY ORDER
Before official printed banknotes appeared in Europe, handwritten paper "money" had long been in use. This note (1665) was addressed by a John Lewis to the London money lenders, Morriss and Clayson, asking them to pay 50 pounds of his money to his servant.

SWEDISH BANKNOTE

In 1661, during a time of shortage of silver coins, the Swedish Stockholm Bank began to issue Europe's first printed paper money. This note (1666) represented 100 dalers (pp. 44–45).

Wax seal

JOHN LAW

The Scotsman John Law was responsible for the issue of paper money in France.

NORWEGIAN MERCHANT'S NOTE

Following the Swedish example, a Norwegian merchant, Jorgen Thor Mohlen, issued printed notes for circulation as money (1695). Mohlen used the coins exchanged to fund his business.

BANK OF SCOTLAND NOTE

During the late 17th century, printed paper money began to be issued in Britain. The Bank of Scotland issued notes valued in Scottish money, like this one dated 1723. Twelve Scottish pounds were equal to one English pound.

FRENCH ROYAL BANKNOTE

It was a Scotsman, John Law, who introduced the idea of printed paper money to France. In 1718, the bank that he had set up in Paris received the French king's approval to issue notes valued in silver coin. However, the bank issued too many notes, and they became worthless.

NEW JERSEY "BILL"

When the British government failed to supply its North American colonies with coins, the colonies decided to issue their own paper money, called bills (p. 48).

ITALIAN PAPAL NOTE

This 31-scudi note of the Bank of the Holy Spirit at Rome was issued in 1786, during the reign of Pope Pius VI, for circulation in the Papal States. The bank, established by Pope Paul V in 1605, was Europe's first national bank.

COMMERCIAL BANKNOTE

Commercial banks have played a large part in the growth of the role of paper money. This note was issued in 1954 in Hong Kong by the Chartered Bank, a London-based commercial bank with branches in every continent.

How coins are made

Millennium
Crown design by
Jeffery Matthews

A COIN IS MADE by marking a blank piece of metal with designs – a process called "minting." The designs are stamped onto the metal by pressing it between two hard metal tools called dies. This basic method of making coins was invented 2,600 years ago, using an anvil and punch as dies (p. 10). Today's dies are part of a large, electrically powered machine press. The blank pieces of metal are also made by electrically powered machines. Current minting techniques are shown here through the production of a Millennium Crown at the British Royal Mint, Llantrisant, Wales.

Pure copper ingot

PLASTER MODEL
Before a coin can be made, an artist creates a design for it. Once the design has been officially approved, it is engraved by hand on a large plaster model. Complex designs make it more difficult for forgers to reproduce every detail.

Time is measured from the Greenwich Meridian, London

Pellets of pure nickel

RECORDING THE DESIGN
Once the plaster model is finalized, a computer records every detail of the surface. A ruby-tipped tracer carefully traces the design in a process that lasts about 20 hours.

Cupro-nickel alloy is cast in a slab, ready to be rolled to the thickness of the coin

MAKING CUPRO-NICKEL
The Millennium Crown is made from an alloy called cupro-nickel. This alloy is made by mixing together pure copper and nickel. Cupro-nickel is often used to make high-denomination coins, because it looks like the silver used in the past to make coins. It is also more hard-wearing than silver.

CHECKING THE DESIGN
After the computer has traced the design, the recorded details are checked on screen for accuracy.

CUTTING THE MASTER PUNCH
The computer record is used to direct an engraving machine that cuts the coin-sized master punch.

Clockface at midnight, New Year's Eve, 1999, represents the start of the new Millennium

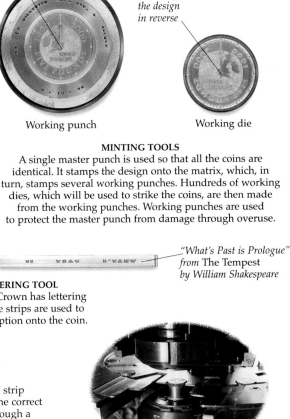

Raised version of the design — Master punch

Matrix

"Incuse" or punched version of the design in reverse

Working punch

Working die

MINTING TOOLS
A single master punch is used so that all the coins are identical. It stamps the design onto the matrix, which, in turn, stamps several working punches. Hundreds of working dies, which will be used to strike the coins, are then made from the working punches. Working punches are used to protect the master punch from damage through overuse.

"What's Past is Prologue" from The Tempest by William Shakespeare

EDGE-LETTERING TOOL
The Millennium Crown has lettering on its edge. These strips are used to impress the inscription onto the coin.

MAKING BLANKS
Once the cupro-nickel strip has been rolled out to the correct thickness, it is passed through a press that stamps the blank coins or "blanks" out of it. The remaining strip, called "scissel," is melted down and used to make more strips.

Fresh-cut blanks

Coin-shaped metal blanks are cut out by a blanking press and then passed through a machine to give them a slightly raised rim

Once the blanks have been cut, the strip is called "scissel"

Rimmed blanks

The rimmed blanks are softened in a special "annealing" furnace and then cleaned.

COINING PRESS
The blank is placed in the coining press, into which the working dies for the front and back of the coin have been fitted. It is then squashed between these dies. It is difficult for anybody to forge coins without this special machinery.

Back (reverse)

Front (obverse)

THE END RESULT
The Millennium Crown has a face value of five pounds and was made by the British Royal Mint to mark the end of the Second Millennium. The crown is "legal tender," so it can be used to buy things, but most people keep it as a souvenir.

How banknotes are made

MAKING BANKNOTES is a secret and complicated business. Banknote printers have to make sure that notes are impossible for forgers to copy easily (pp. 18–19). Some of the less-secret techniques used are revealed here through the work of the world's busiest banknote printers. The company often makes specimen notes, like this example, to show the range of techniques to its customers. There are four main stages involved: design, papermaking, ink-mixing, and printing by lithography, intaglio, and letterpress.

COMPUTER DESIGN
After an artist has created the design for a banknote, it is perfected on screen using a specially developed computer program. Then color sample proofs are printed out for approval. Once the design is finalized, the different printings are separated on a computer before the lithography printing plates are made.

Sharp engraving tools called burins are used for cutting the design into the plate

A burnisher is used for smoothing the flat surface

MAGNIFYING GLASS
The engraver needs a magnifying glass to work on the tiny details of the design that make it hard for a forger to copy the note.

ENGRAVER AT WORK
The engraver uses traditional tools to hand cut the fine details of a design onto a steel plate over a period of several weeks.

Reflecting green

Reflecting red

PAPER QUALITY
Notes are printed on paper made from cotton fibers. Only paper of this quality is strong enough to stand the wear and tear of daily use. It often contains security thread to deter forgery.

SECURITY THREAD
Plastic thread embedded in the paper cannot be successfully photocopied since its color varies from red to green under the light. When photocopied it simply looks black.

INTAGLIO PRINTING PLATE
The main design of most banknotes is usually printed using a design that has been hand-engraved on a steel plate. This example shows a portrait of Thomas de la Rue, founder of De La Rue, the banknote printing firm.

INTAGLIO PROOF
When the intaglio plate is inked, the ink fills the engraved design. The plate is then printed under high pressure onto the paper, raising an inked impression of the design, which can be felt by fingertip. Some banks use this technique to add identification marks for people with limited vision.

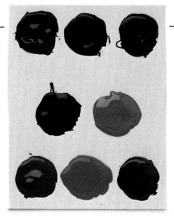

Rainbow-shift
proof No. 2

Rainbow-shift
proof No. 1

Proof showing
combined printing of
background design

BANKNOTE PAPER
Most banknotes have a watermark design molded into the paper. The watermark shows best when the note is held up to the light. On many modern notes, the security thread appears and disappears between the watermarked bars. These bars can be felt by fingertip – a useful aid for people with limited vision.

Ultraviolet-sensitive
ink proof

*Security thread
with microtext*

*Playing card symbols refer to
De La Rue's printing of playing
cards in the 19th century*

COLOR PROOFS
The background design is printed by a system called offset lithography. The design is separated by computer into three groups of colors, which are recombined in the printing process. The inks are transferred onto a single rubber-covered cylinder that prints the combined image.

THE END RESULT
A different method of printing called letterpress is used to print official signatures and to add a different serial number to each banknote. De La Rue uses specimens like this "house note" to show its customers the latest security features developed to protect notes from being forged. They will be demonstrated to banks in countries as far apart as Singapore, Kenya, Jordan, Jamaica, and Ecuador, as well as to banks in the United Kingdom, the Channel Islands, and Europe.

Forgeries and fakes

Imprisonment is the most common form of punishment for forgers caught in the act today, but heavy fines are also imposed.

Fᴏʀɢᴇʀʏ, ᴛʜᴇ ᴀʀᴛ ᴏғ ᴍᴀᴋɪɴɢ ғᴀʟꜱᴇ ᴍᴏɴᴇʏ, has always been considered a very serious crime. In the past, punishments for forgery included being deported, having your hands cut off, and being executed! However, driven on by the profit to be made by turning inexpensive pieces of metal or paper into something of value, forgers continue to break the law, although these days the punishment is more likely to be a large fine or imprisonment. Not only do forgers harm the individuals taken in by their deceit, they also cheat the state by whose authority money is issued. Despite all the devices adopted by coinmakers (pp. 14–15) and banknote printers (pp. 16–17) to make forgeries very difficult, there are still plenty of forgers prepared to overcome these difficulties, take the risks, and, if caught, face the consequences!

PLATED FORGERIES
These copies of gold Greek coins were made from gold-plated copper. They were recognized as forgeries when the plating cracked to reveal the green copper underneath.

Silver case

Tin disk

Round half-crown coin cut to the shape of a 50-pence piece

Genuine coin

Lead cast

COPIES
The two copies of a British 50-pence were meant to deceive those not familiar with the new coin. One is made from lead, the other is cut from an old, round coin.

TIN DOLLAR
This Chinese forgery of a Mexican silver dollar, found in Shanghai in the 1930s, was made by enclosing a tin disk in a thin silver case.

Nonexistent bank

NONEXISTENT BANK
When Italy was short of small change during the 1970s (p. 37), some Italian banks made small-change notes. An enterprising forger printed his own notes, but in the name of a bank that did not exist!

HANDRAWN FORGERY
All the details on this false Swedish 10-daler banknote of 1868 were copied by hand. This was undoubtedly a time-consuming but presumably profitable task for the forger!

The first note is a forgery of the 1835 Bank of Rome note on the far right (both reduced). The forger copied most of the details (including the words at the bottom that say "the law punishes forgers"), but his mistakes enabled his crime to be detected. How many can you spot?

THE HANGMAN'S NOOSE
This cartoon (reduced) is in the form of a Bank of England note. It criticizes the severe punishment for using forged notes, and shows Britannia (the bank's emblem) eating children, and the pound sign as a hangman's noose.

Checking change

In order to protect themselves from losing money by receiving a forged coin or note, traders have always been very careful to check all the money paid to them. When money was in the form of gold and silver coins, the best precaution was to check that the gold or silver was of good quality, and that each coin contained the full weight of precious metal. There were various ways of doing this.

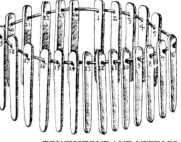

TOUCHSTONE AND NEEDLES
To check the quality of a gold coin, a trader would mark the black touchstone with the equivalent gold carat touch needle (above), and then compare that mark with the mark the coin left. The streaks here (left to right) were made with 24-, 9-, 12-, 15-, 18-, and 22-carat gold.

24-carat gold coin

Punch to test whether coin was plated

Greek silver coin, 5th century

Portuguese Indian coin, 1688

CHECKED COINS
In order to be sure that a coin was not plated, traders would cut into the surface, as has been done on this Greek coin. The Indian coin has been checked with small engraved punches.

DIRECTIONS for using M.S. HENRY'S,
Royal Patent Ballance & Gauge for **Gold Coin of the last & present Reign,**
(Agreeable to the *last Regulation.)*

1ly Put your Coin in the swinging Pan and to weigh a Guinea slide the weight home to the end of the Beam; for a Half Guinea advance it forward home to the small Pin, then press the Brass Laver in the middle & the weight will be determined; the Quarter Guinea is weighed the same as the Half-

Guinea by putting the Quarter Guinea weight in the Pan with the Quarter Guinea. — 2ly Apply your Coin to the Gauge, the large stroke for the Guinea, the middle one for the Half and the small one for the Quarter d? if they Pass through (on turning them all round) be affurd they are not Counterfeits. pr 16. 6d

Sold in London, Wholesale, by James Stamp, Goldsmith, Cheapside, Woolley, and Heming Hardwaremen Cheapside, Stibbs, and Deane, Hardwaremen, Fish Street Hill.

COIN BALANCE AND WEIGHTS
This British balance scale was used in the 18th century to weigh gold coins. The brass weights above are from 17th-century Belgium, and are varied so that foreign gold coins imported into the area from the Netherlands, France, England, Scotland, Italy, Portugal, Hungary, and Morocco could be weighed.

A plated coin of the right weight would be too thick to go through this slot

Money and trade

MONEY IS at the center of trade, whether it takes place in a local store or on the international commodities (products) market. Money, the "medium of exchange," enables both buyer and seller to agree to part with what they have in order to get what they want. In the days when money took the form of precious metals such as gold and silver, heavy chests of coins were shipped around the world in trade! However, sometimes the money itself stayed still, but the ownership of it was transferred by pieces of paper called bills of exchange. Today, money rarely moves in trade. Although bills of exchange are still in use, most international payments are made by telephone and computer (pp. 60–61).

DUTCH TRADERS' MANUAL
During the 16th century, so many foreign coins were handled by Dutch merchants that they used handbooks to identify current coins from other lands and to indicate their value. The one here was published in Antwerp in 1580. These pages show Scandinavian silver dalers (pp. 42–45).

OWLS EVERYWHERE!
The silver coins of Athens (right) were known as "owls" because of their design; the Little Owl was the special bird of the goddess Athena. Athens was the richest city of Ancient Greece, and traded throughout the world with its silver coins. The design was so popular that many countries issued coins with a similar design, as you can see from this map.

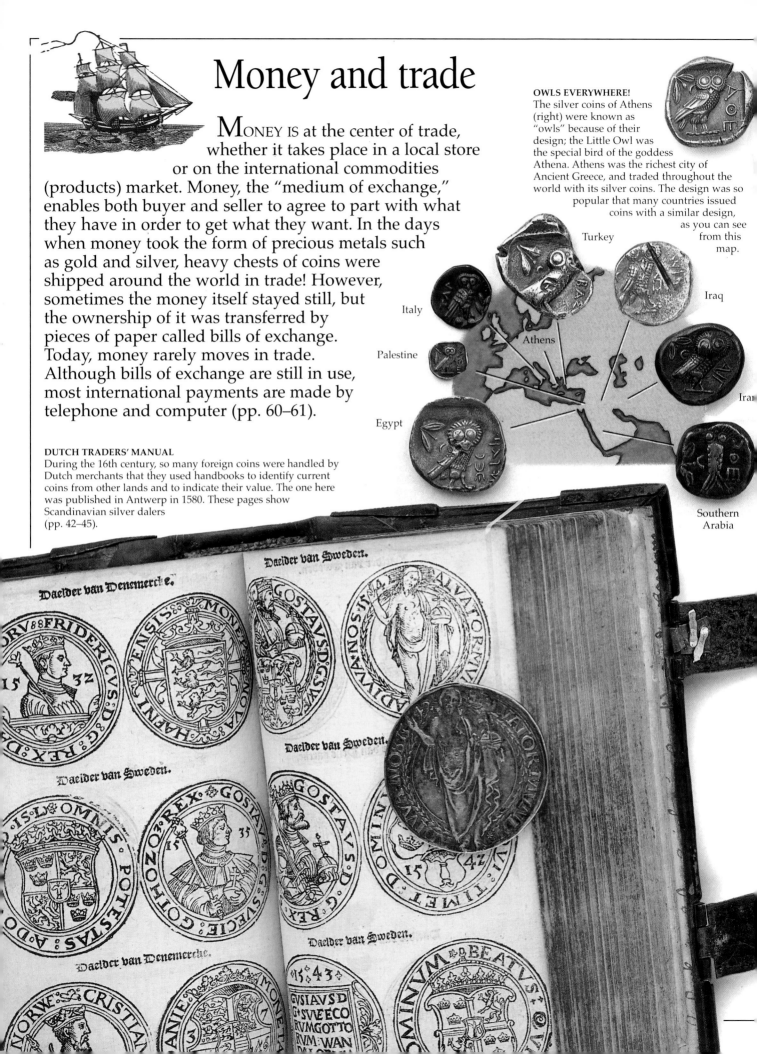

Turkey

Italy

Iraq

Athens

Palestine

Iran

Egypt

Southern Arabia

Daelder van Denemercke.

Daelder van Sweden.

Daelder van Sweden.

Daelder van Sweden.

Daelder van Denemercke.

Daelder van Sweden.

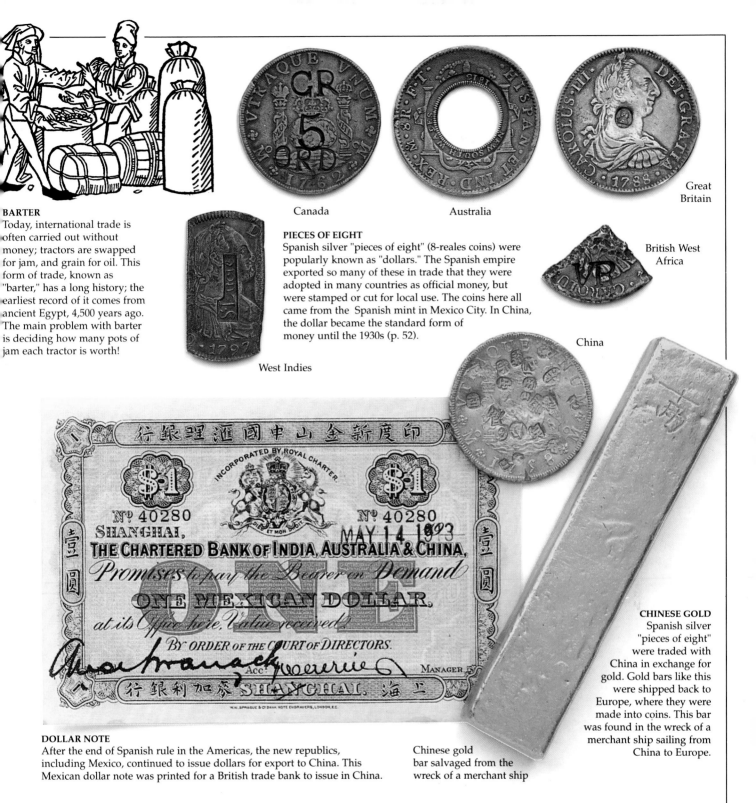

BARTER
Today, international trade is often carried out without money; tractors are swapped for jam, and grain for oil. This form of trade, known as "barter," has a long history; the earliest record of it comes from ancient Egypt, 4,500 years ago. The main problem with barter is deciding how many pots of jam each tractor is worth!

Canada

Australia

Great Britain

PIECES OF EIGHT
Spanish silver "pieces of eight" (8-reales coins) were popularly known as "dollars." The Spanish empire exported so many of these in trade that they were adopted in many countries as official money, but were stamped or cut for local use. The coins here all came from the Spanish mint in Mexico City. In China, the dollar became the standard form of money until the 1930s (p. 52).

British West Africa

West Indies

China

DOLLAR NOTE
After the end of Spanish rule in the Americas, the new republics, including Mexico, continued to issue dollars for export to China. This Mexican dollar note was printed for a British trade bank to issue in China.

Chinese gold bar salvaged from the wreck of a merchant ship

CHINESE GOLD
Spanish silver "pieces of eight" were traded with China in exchange for gold. Gold bars like this were shipped back to Europe, where they were made into coins. This bar was found in the wreck of a merchant ship sailing from China to Europe.

BILL OF EXCHANGE
Coins are no longer used in international trade, and money is usually paid by telephone messages between bank computers or by written instructions like this bill of exchange. A bill of exchange is a written order signed by one trader instructing a second person, or bank, to pay from his account a specified amount in a specified currency to the other trader by a specified date.

Money in war

ALEXANDER THE GREAT
This silver coin (slightly enlarged) was made by Alexander the Great in 326 B.C. to commemorate his victory over an Indian king. The king is on an elephant.

SIEGE GOLD
During the siege of Athens by the Spartans in 406 B.C., silver owl coins (p. 20) ran out. The Athenians had to melt down golden statues of the goddess of victory to make these coins!

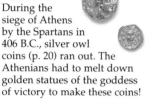

THROUGHOUT HISTORY, money and war seem to have marched along hand in hand. Money plays a large part in the preparations for war, since it pays for the necessary arms and buys the services of mercenaries, professional soldiers who will fight for any country that pays them enough. The hardships of war have led to the issue of new forms of money in cities under siege (cut off and surrounded by the enemy) as well as by governments that have run out of money. The same circumstances have also brought into circulation unofficial forms of money such as cigarettes. Too often money provides the reward for success in war; in the past, soldiers have frequently been recruited on the understanding that they would be paid from the booty captured from the enemy.

SIEGE NOTE
When a Prussian army besieged French revolutionary forces in the German city of Mainz in 1793, the French army issued "emergency" notes for use within the city. These notes were of French denomination.

CHARLES I OF ENGLAND
Charles I issued this coin in 1644 at his Oxford mint after the Roundheads, his opponents in Parliament, took over his London mint.

During the English Civil War (1642–1648), the Cavaliers fought the Roundheads for control of the country

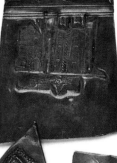

SIEGE SILVER
In 1644, Cavaliers (royalist troops) besieged in Scarborough Castle in northern England cut up silver plates to make coins. The castle and denomination were stamped on each coin.

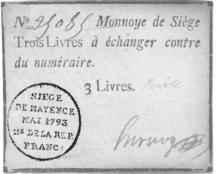

CONFEDERATE NOTES
In 1864, during the American Civil War, the southern Confederate States financed the war by issuing notes to be repaid in coin two years after the war ended.

Confederate forces, flag flying, storm a Yankee-held fort during the American Civil War

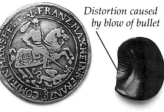
Distortion caused by blow of bullet

BOER WAR BADGES
These patriotic badges show the British Commander-in-Chief, Lord Roberts (top), and one of his officers, Colonel Baden-Powell (below), who issued the Mafeking siege notes. Baden-Powell later founded the Boy Scout movement.

LIFE SAVERS!
During Europe's Thirty Years War (1618–1648), many German soldiers carried a St. George thaler (top left) because they believed it would stop bullets. At the Battle of Culloden, Scotland, an English soldier was saved from death by the copper halfpenny (right), which bears the mark of the bullet it deflected.

Boer coins

BOER WAR MONEY
Emergency issues of money were made by both the Boers (Dutch settlers in South Africa) and the British during the Boer war in South Africa (1899–1902). In 1900, the British, besieged by the Boers at Mafeking, issued notes like the one above. After losing Pretoria (the capital city) and their mint, the Boers retreated and issued gold pound coins from a blacksmith's shop.

WAR BOOTY
This Mexican silver dollar, mounted to be worn as a medal, was part of the booty captured from a German ship by an Australian crew in 1914.

Mount inscribed "Nov 9 1914 HMAS SYDNEY and SMS EMDEN"

REVOLUTIONARY NOTE
A large issue of notes, like the one above for 10 pesos, was made in 1900 by the treasury at the province of Ocana in Colombia, South America, to pay soldiers serving in the revolutionary army of General Urribe.

"FROM FRED TO NELLIE"

A British soldier made this coin into a keepsake for his wife when he left to fight in France during World War I.

DESERT RAT MONEY
Allied troops serving in Libya (North Africa) during World War II were paid in Italian lire notes, the currency of this former Italian colony.

SMOKE OR SPEND?
At the end of World War II, a shortage of coins and notes in Europe meant that other desirable objects were used as money. Cigarettes, food, and clothing, all in short supply, became acceptable means of payment. Unfortunately, there was no Hammurabi's column (p. 6) to fix a scale of payments.

GREEK OCCUPATION MONEY
Italian lire were also used in Greece by the occupying Italian army. On this note, issued in 1944 for use on the Greek island of Rhodes, you can see the Roman twins Romulus and Remus and the wolf that suckled them, as well as pictures of two coins from ancient Rhodes.

The power of money

IT HAS BEEN SAID that the love of money is the root of all evil, and it certainly seems to be for some people; misers love their own money, and thieves love other people's! Money has led many people into crime but, curiously, money also has the reputation of bringing luck. Who can deny the obvious increase in good fortune of those who have a lot of it! There are many curious beliefs about the power of money for good. Since ancient times, coins have been used to drive off demons, to ensure a safe journey after death, to cure the plague, to protect in battle, and to promise everlasting love.

KING MIDAS
Perhaps the most famous story of greed is the legend of King Midas, who asked the gods to give him the ability to turn all he touched into gold. It was not a kind gift, as he soon discovered. His pleasure turned to pain as food, drink, and, finally, his favorite daughter also turned to gold!

The Phoenician god Melqart appears on the front of these silver shekels

The root of all evil

Murder, robbery, arson, and bribery – where there is crime, there is money. Money itself is surely not evil; it is nothing more than a necessary part of everyday life. So why does it so often appear as the motive for crime? Are greed and envy, or poverty and need the causes, or is it because criminals see in money the means of achieving the good fortune they seem to lack?

COIN CLIPPINGS
Before the invention of coinmaking machines, coins were not perfectly round. It was easy to trim a bit off the edge of silver coins for melting down without anyone noticing, so that the coins could still be spent. These coils were clipped from silver English coins in the late 17th century. During William III's reign (1689-1702), people were executed in London for this crime.

BEWARE. . . PIRATES!
Spanish treasure fleets shipping silver "pieces of eight" and gold doubloons from Mexico to Europe (pp. 38–39) were the main target of pirates. As they had few opportunities to spend their loot, pirates often buried their treasure, saving it for their "retirement fund"!

Keepsake for a child who died aged 18 months

MARY RAMSHAW BORN MAY 4 -1773- AGED 18 MONTHS DIED OCT 10 1774

Hearts and doves symbolizing love

LOVE TOKENS AND KEEPSAKES
In Britain and America, it used to be the custom for engaged couples to exchange coins as pledges of their love (top). Tokens were also made as keepsakes of dead loved ones (center), an exiled convict (bottom), or to commemorate a birth (right).

These coins were issued by the Chinese emperor Kangxi, and the characters of his name, meaning health and prosperity, appear on the coins

THIRTY PIECES OF SILVER
One of the world's most famous crimes, the betrayal of Jesus by one of his followers, Judas, had its cash reward: 30 pieces of silver. The coins in question are thought to have been silver shekels from the Phoenician city of Tyre. Tyrian shekels were the only silver coins available in quantity in 1st-century Palestine.

ARE YOU A MISER?
Looking after your money is no bad thing (p. 58), but if you become so mean that you will not spend any of it either on yourself or others, then you have undoubtedly become a victim of the power of money!

Demon-dispelling sword for driving off a fever demon

Red is a lucky color for the Chinese

Corpse hands over his fare to Charon the ferryman

HEALING SWORD AND COINS
This demon-dispelling Chinese coin sword was made to hang above the bed of sick people to ward off evil spirits. Instead of a sword, a coin-shaped exorcism charm (top right) could be used. In Britain, monarchs gave sick subjects a gold coin (center) to help cure them. In Germany, silver medals like the one to the right were thought to protect owners from the plague.

Money, myth, and magic

It is not difficult to see why money is seen as a source of good fortune. Until we look closely, rich people always seem to be blessed with all the good fortune they need. They can afford to buy all of the material goods they need to make their life happy. However, there is a more magical, spiritual side to money. The pictures and words on coins often add to their "power" to bring good luck.

"ANY FARES PLEASE"?
According to mythology, the ancient Greeks put a silver coin, "obol," into the mouth of a corpse to pay Charon, the ferryman, to take the corpse across the Styx River into Hades. The coin (left) was found in the mouth of a Persian corpse.

This note claims to be an issue of the Bank of Hell

HOLY COINS
Travelers wore the silver coin charm (top left) to gain the protection of St. George, patron saint of horsemen. Indian Muslims carried the name of Mohammed on the copy of a square silver rupee (top right). The image of the monkey god, Hanuman, on the round silver rupee (right) gave comfort to Hindus.

HELL BANK NOTE
№A15917248 冥通銀行 №A15917248
伍仟萬

DOLLARS

FIFTY MILLION DOLLARS

50000000

HELL MONEY
The Chinese send money to their dead ancestors by regularly burning special banknotes like the one here.

The monkey god, Hanuman, guardian of those in need

One million dollars!

A STICKY BUSINESS
A Penny Black stamp like the one above could cost anything between $240 and $4,700, depending on its condition. However, a Penny Blue is even more valuable; you could expect to pay between $500 and $9,350 for one of those.

Roman coin of the Emperor Diocletian, (A.D. 284–305)

Queen Anne coin (1703) made from captured Spanish treasure

IF YOU WERE suddenly to become a millionaire, what would you do with your newly acquired wealth? Would you rush out and spend it all right away? Would you plan carefully what you were going to do with it all – perhaps investing some and saving the rest for the future? Or would you save it all, never spending or giving any of it away? If you were to rush out to the stores to spend it, you might find that it is more difficult than you imagined! Like many young millionaires, you could spend much of it on designer clothes, records, tapes, computers, stereos, and vacations, but you would still have a lot left.

Ancient Greek coin, (c. 460 B.C.)

RARE COINS
These three coins (actual size) are worth thousands of dollars each. The Roman gold coin (top left), the English gold five-guinea coin of Queen Anne (top right), and the ancient Greek silver 10-drachma coin (bottom) are valuable because they are rare. However, you do not need to be a millionaire to collect coins (pp. 60–61).

STACKS OF MONEY
There are 10,000 one-hundred dollar bills in this pile – a total of $1 million. The Sultan of Brunei is believed to be the richest man in the world – his fortune is estimated at around $25 billion.

Display board showing latest bid in five currencies

GOING, GOING, GONE!
People can spend a lot of money in an auction room – often much more than they intended to. The bid for the painting in this picture has reached $97,260 – almost one-tenth of the stack of dollars on this page.

Modern gambling chips

MONTE CARLO MADNESS
Some people enjoy gambling with their money. For them, the excitement of playing games of chance to increase their fortune is often an addiction. Even if they lose, they still dream of winning a fortune. Monte Carlo, Monaco, a town in southeastern France, is perhaps the most famous gambling center for the rich. This gambling chip is for one million francs, and would have been used in the 1930s.

The roll of dice can win or lose a fortune

If you are smart, or lucky, at cards, your fortune may grow. If you are not smart, or unlucky, it may disappear altogether!

FINE WINE?
Buying old wine is a gamble not many people are willing to try. The wine of Château Lafite is famous, and a bottle of 1902 vintage like this would cost around $600 at auction. However, there is a high risk that wine that old will be totally undrinkable, so most collectors prefer to leave the bottle unopened; it seems that they derive enough satisfaction from just looking at the bottle to justify such an expense!

MIS EN BOUTEILLES AU CHÂTEAU

CHATEAU LAFITE-ROTHSCHILD
1902

APPELLATION PAUILLAC CONTRÔLÉE

Shared currencies

THE EURO SYMBOL
A new symbol was created for the introduction of the euro in 1999. It copies the double bar of the pound and dollar signs.

W HEN TWO OR MORE governments decide to share a common currency, the result is known as a monetary union. The earliest monetary unions can be traced back to about 450 B.C. in Ancient Greece, while the most recent is the introduction of the euro in many European countries in 1999. In the past, monetary unions also came into being when a particular form of currency, like Indian silver rupees, did so well that its use spread to more than one state. One modern example of this is the everyday use of the US dollar in many parts of the world.

Byzantine Ummayad

RIVALS UNITED
The Christian Byzantine Empire and its rival, the Muslim Ummayad Caliphate, used the same denomination gold coin, based on the *solidus* of the former Roman Empire. The Byzantine coin has the head of Christ; the Ummayad coin has the declaration of the Islamic faith.

Latin Monetary Union

A forerunner of the European Economic and Monetary Union, the Latin Monetary Union was established by France, with Belgium, Italy, Switzerland, and Greece in 1865. Members kept their own currency name and coin and note designs, but they all used a common standard unit of currency. Other countries later aligned their currencies to this standard.

Swiss franc

Belgian franc

French franc

Portrait of Napoleon III

Italian lira

Greek drachma

GOLD AND SILVER
The standard gold and silver coins of the members of the Latin union matched each other in size and weight, but each country used its own denomination system.

NAPOLEON III
Napoleon III and his government sought to make trade easier through the introduction in 1865 of a new international standard based on the value of gold.

Chinese cash

Javanese cash

CHINESE EXPORTS
From the tenth century A.D., Chinese coins were exported in such large numbers to the other countries of the Far East that most of them adopted the Chinese cash coins as their standard currency. By the 15th century, Chinese coins were used in Java, India, and East Africa. In many countries, local copies of the cash were also made

African Union

In Africa, the trading activities of European imperial powers led to the circulation of foreign currencies. Some powers, such as France, established a common monetary system in all of the countries that they ruled.

FRENCH AFRICA
France set up two monetary unions based on the franc in its Central and Western territories. These are still used in the former colonies today.

German rupee

Italian rupee

COMMON COINS
British, German, Portuguese, and Italian colonies in East Africa all issued coins based on the British Indian silver rupee.

25 franc note, West African States

100 franc note, Central African States

European Economic and Monetary Union

The euro was introduced in 1999 into 11 of the states belonging to the European Union (EU). This marked the start of the European Economic and Monetary Union, which was formed to strengthen the economic power and unity of the EU. Banknotes and coins denominated in euros and cents were then prepared to replace the former national currencies in 2002.

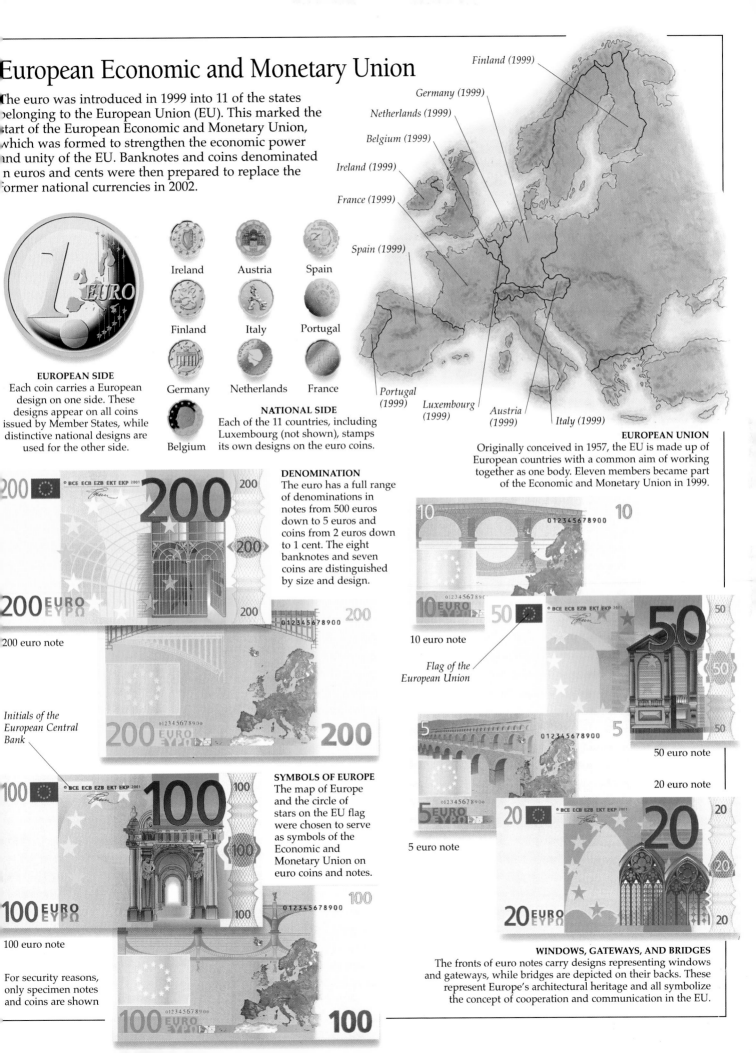

Finland (1999)
Germany (1999)
Netherlands (1999)
Belgium (1999)
Ireland (1999)
France (1999)
Spain (1999)
Portugal (1999)
Luxembourg (1999)
Austria (1999)
Italy (1999)

Ireland Austria Spain
Finland Italy Portugal
Germany Netherlands France
Belgium

EUROPEAN SIDE
Each coin carries a European design on one side. These designs appear on all coins issued by Member States, while distinctive national designs are used for the other side.

NATIONAL SIDE
Each of the 11 countries, including Luxembourg (not shown), stamps its own designs on the euro coins.

EUROPEAN UNION
Originally conceived in 1957, the EU is made up of European countries with a common aim of working together as one body. Eleven members became part of the Economic and Monetary Union in 1999.

DENOMINATION
The euro has a full range of denominations in notes from 500 euros down to 5 euros and coins from 2 euros down to 1 cent. The eight banknotes and seven coins are distinguished by size and design.

200 euro note

Initials of the European Central Bank

10 euro note

Flag of the European Union

50 euro note

20 euro note

SYMBOLS OF EUROPE
The map of Europe and the circle of stars on the EU flag were chosen to serve as symbols of the Economic and Monetary Union on euro coins and notes.

5 euro note

100 euro note

For security reasons, only specimen notes and coins are shown

WINDOWS, GATEWAYS, AND BRIDGES
The fronts of euro notes carry designs representing windows and gateways, while bridges are depicted on their backs. These represent Europe's architectural heritage and all symbolize the concept of cooperation and communication in the EU.

France

TODAY, FRANCE'S MONEY consists of francs divided into centimes. The oldest known French money is Greek silver coins made in Massilia (Marseilles) almost 2,500 years ago. From the 2nd century B.C., the Gauls (Celtic peoples of ancient France) issued coins that copied Greek designs, but when the Romans conquered the Gauls, they brought their own coins with them. Roman coin designs remained in use until the German Frankish kings, who overthrew the Romans, began to issue silver deniers, the first truly French coins. The franc, first issued as a gold coin in 1360, and as a silver coin in 1577, did not become the main unit of French currency until 1795. Its value has changed many times since then as the result of revolutions and war. The last major change was in 1960, when a new franc was issued worth 100 of the previously used francs.

The Greek goddess Artemis (p. 10)

PATRON SAINT OF COINMAKERS
St. Eligius, the patron saint of coinmakers and goldsmiths, worked at the Paris mint during the 7th century for the Merovingian kings of Gaul. In this stained-glass panel he is shown using traditional tools for making coins (p. 10).

CELTIC GOLD
The head of the Greek god Apollo on this gold coin (100 B.C.) was copied by the Celts from an earlier Greek coin.

Back

GREEK SILVER COINS
During the 5th century B.C., the Greek colony at Massilia issued small silver coins with various designs, like the small coin at the top with the ram's head. The colony was extremely prosperous, and from about 350 B.C., its silver coins were widely used by the Celtic peoples of Gaul and northern Italy.

Prow of Roman galley

Front

CELTIC WARRIOR
On this silver coin of the Roman Republic, a lifelike portrait of a Gaulish chief appears on the front and his war chariot appears on the back. The coin was made in about 48 B.C., soon after Julius Caesar conquered Gaul.

ROMAN GAUL COIN
The letters "CI V" on this coin stand for "Colonia Julia Viennensis," which means the "Colony of Julius Caesar at Vienne." Vienne is in the south of France; this coin was made there around 36 B.C.

Louis XIV chose the sun as his emblem because he saw himself as the all-powerful center of the universe

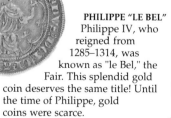

PHILIPPE "LE BEL"
Philippe IV, who reigned from 1285–1314, was known as "le Bel," the Fair. This splendid gold coin deserves the same title! Until the time of Philippe, gold coins were scarce.

SILVER DENIER AND GROS
Charlemagne (742–814) issued this denier (left). The denier was introduced by his father, Pepin, the first king of France. It was virtually the only denomination used in France until the introduction of the silver gros (right) by King Louis IX in 1266.

"LUD" is the abbreviation of "Ludivicus," the Latin form of "Louis"

SILVER EC
From the time of Francis (1515–1547), portraits of th kings of France appeare on coins. King Louis XI (the "Sun King") appear on this écu (left). Th European Economi Community has recentl revived the name EC (European Currency Uni for its new commo currency uni

The denomination "sol" was popularly known as "sou"

REVOLUTIONARY PAPER MONEY

From 1790 until 1793, the French Revolution was funded by issues of paper money known as "assignats" (left). Coins like those on the right continued to be issued using the pre-revolutionary denominations, but the designs were changed to reflect the political situation. The franc became the main unit of currency in 1795.

Five-livre coin of Louis XVI issued in 1792, the year before his execution on the guillotine

Royal portrait is replaced by the figures of Hercules, Liberty, and Equality on this five-franc coin of 1795

First Republic, 1792–1804

Second Republic, 1848–1852

Napoleon Bonaparte's portrait appeared on coins from 1802 when he was made Consul of the Republic. He became Emperor in 1804

Third Republic, 1871–1940

MONEY TO BURN

Because far too many "assignats" were issued, the notes became worthless. In 1796, the printing presses were destroyed, and the notes burned.

FIVE MARIANNES

From 1793, the main design of French Republican coinage has been a female head representing the Republic. The image became popularly known as "Marianne." She is normally shown wearing the cap of liberty, or a wreath. Many different versions have been used; the five here are found on coins of the five Republics.

Fifth Republic, 1958–present day

Fourth Republic, 1945–1958

Distinctive raised mark for recognition by those with impaired sight

Metallic ink security feature

LOCAL PAPER MONEY

During World War I, and for a few years after, most small change was issued locally. Both coins and notes, like this 50-centimes note of Grenoble, were issued by local trade associations.

COMMEMORATIVE COIN

Commemorative coins are frequently issued for general circulation. This 1988 franc celebrates the 30th anniversary of the election of Charles de Gaulle as President.

TODAY'S MONEY

Since January 1, 1999, the euro has been the official currency of France, replacing the French franc. Euro notes and coins circulate from January 1, 2002, replacing the franc coins and notes.

FF20 FF10

FF5 FF2 FF1

20c 10c 5c

Germany

UNTIL THE INTRODUCTION of the euro on January 1, 1999, the currency of Germany was the mark, even when Germany was divided between 1945 and 1990. The mark, divided into 100 pfennigs, was introduced in 1871 when the German Empire was formed by Wilhelm I, King of Prussia. Before it became the main unit of currency, the mark was used as a weight. The main currencies were the thaler, the gulden, and the ducat. The pfennig has a longer history, and was the name used for German silver coins of the 11th century. Before the Empire was established, the German kingdoms, states, and cities each had their own currency system. Similar coinage systems existed in the neighboring areas of Poland, Austria, and Switzerland.

This engraving shows a Mint Master weighing out coins in the 14th century

ROMAN GOLD
This large gold coin was made at the mint in Trier to reward soldiers serving the Roman emperor Constantius I. Britannia kneels before him as he is crowned by Victory, a Roman goddess.

Conrad II, King of Saxony (1024–1039)

SILVER PFENNIGS
Early pfennigs, like the one at the top, used French and English designs, but during the 12th century, many original German designs appeared on broader, thinner versions. The coin on the left is an issue of Emperor Frederick I Barbarossa (1152–1190), and the coin on the right was issued by Otto I of Brandenburg (1157–1184).

In this 15th-century Swiss drawing, you can see coinmakers minting small silver pfennigs

Coin issued in Rhenish Palatine showing St. John the Baptist

Coin issued in Trier showing St. Peter

Coin issued in Basel showing the Virgin Mary

GOLD GULDEN
Gold coins began to be issued in quantity during the 14th century. They were the same size as Italian florins (p. 36).

Thaler of Count Stephen of Slick, 1519

Thaler of Johan Wilhelm, Duke of Saxony, 1569

The arm of God crowns the horse

FREDERICK THE GREAT OF PRUSSIA
Frederick, the Philosopher King (1740–1786), reorganized his coinage system so that it was based on the thaler and the pfennig. This gold coin struck at Berlin in 1750 was worth 10 thalers.

SILVER THALERS
During the 15th century, the discovery of large silver mines in Joachimsthal in Bohemia (now called Austria) led to the issue of new, large, silver coins. These were called Joachimsthalers, "thalers" for short. The word "dollar" is the English version of this name. The silver from the Bohemian mines was exported throughout western Europe.

The horse leaping over the silver mines is the symbol of Luneburg

Four-thaler coin of Christian Ludwig, Duke of Brunswick-Luneburg, 1662

FIVE-MARK NOTE
When Wilhelm I of Prussia became the Emperor (Kaiser) of Germany in 1871, the German monetary system was unified, with the mark as the main unit of currency. The former thaler was equal to five marks.

Coins made of iron

STACKS OF MONEY
During 1923, the German monetary system descended into chaos and banknotes became worthless. As well as using notes as wallpaper, parents gave bundles to children to play with!

LOCAL MONEY
During and after World War I, small-change coins and notes were issued by local authorities.

ZERO MADNESS
Because the mark became more and more worthless after World War I, people needed more marks to buy goods. To keep up with this, banks issued notes with high denominations, like this Cologne 200 million mark note. Bank clerks went insane dealing with the ever-increasing number of zeros!

EAST GERMAN 10-PFENNIG
Before the unification of Germany, East and West had separate currencies. The backs of the East German coins have designs representing labor and agriculture. The back of this 10-pfennig coin displays a cogged wheel of industry and an ear of wheat to represent agriculture.

Design showing cogged wheel and ear of corn

DM5   DM2   DM1

Pf50   Pf10

TODAY'S MONEY
The euro replaced the Deutsche mark as the currency of Germany on January 1, 1999. Euro notes and coins circulate starting 2002.

Netherlands and Belgium

Detail from "The Moneylender and his wife" by the Flemish painter, Quentin Massys

THE MODERN CURRENCIES of the Netherlands and Belgium were established when they became kingdoms. In 1815, the Kingdom of the United Netherlands – which at that time included Belgium – kept its former gulden currency, but reorganized it as a decimal system divided into 100 cents. When the Belgian kingdom became independent from the Netherlands in 1830, it adopted the franc from France, the country that had ruled both countries during the earlier Napoleonic period. Coinage had originally been introduced by the Celts into this area in the second century B.C. It then developed further under Roman, German, French, Spanish, and British influence. From the 13th century, the Netherlands and Belgium were the center of international trade, and many foreign coins circulated there (pp. 20–21).

BELGIAN GOLD
This is an example of the earliest Belgian coins made by the Celtic tribe called the Nervii. These coins have also been found in the Netherlands

MEROVINGIAN GOLD
The mint of Duursted is named on the earliest Dutch coins. It is spelled DORESTAT on this gold coin of the Merovingian kings

Gold lion of Philip le Bon, Duke of Burgundy (1419–1467)

Dutch gold ducat of Rudolph, Bishop of Utrecht (1423–1455)

Belgian silver gros of Adolf, Bishop of Liege (1313–1344)

LOCAL COINS
From the 11th to 16th centuries, many local gold and silver coins were issued in Belgium and the Netherlands. The largest issues were by the Dukes of Burgundy, but local religious leaders, nobles, and towns also issued their own coins.

SIEGE MONEY
These coins are emergency issues of cities involved in the revolt of the Dutch United Provinces, which began in 1568 against their Spanish rulers.

Lion of Holland countermark added to Spanish coins by order of William Prince of Orange in 1573

Cardboard coin made when Leiden was besieged by the Spanish army (1574)

Bundle of arrows represents the Dutch United Provinces

Silver coin made by the Spanish governor of Amsterdam while under attack by the Dutch (1578)

SPANISH OR FREE?
The mint of the Duchy of Gelderland produced both of these Dutch gold coins. The coin on the left was issued by the Spanish king, Philip II, in 1560. The coin on the right was struck by independent Gelderland in the name of the United Provinces in 1616.

EARL OF LEICESTER
The English Earl of Leicester, acting for Elizabeth I, Queen of England, supported the Dutch revolt against Spain. In 1586, he attempted to reorganize the Dutch coinage system

Isabella and her husband, Archduke Albert of Austria

THE PORT OF AMSTERDAM
During the 16th century, many wealthy merchants lived in Amsterdam since it was one of the busiest trading cities in the world. The town is cut by some 40 canals, which are crossed by about 400 bridges.

DOUBLE SOVEREIGN
In 1598, Philip II of Spain handed over his Dutch and Belgian possessions to his daughter Isabella and her husband, Archduke Albert of Austria. This gold coin was made at the Brussels mint in 1618.

This Dutch "daalder" (Dutch version of "dollar") coin copied the Spanish "piece of eight" from Mexico

TRADE AND EMPIRE
A variety of forms of money was made for the Dutch empire established during the 17th century. This silver daalder was made in Amsterdam in 1601 for trade with the Far East, and the copper bar coin was made in Ceylon in 1785. The gulden note was issued by the Javasche Bank in the Dutch East Indies in 1920.

THE CONGO RIVER
The only trade route into the Belgian Congo was along the great Congo River.

French coin

Flemish coin

BILINGUAL COINS
Because Belgium has two official languages, French and Flemish, two separate sets of coins are now issued. Previously, some coins had both languages on the same coin.

CONGO FRANC
In 1885, the Belgian king became ruler of a part of Central Africa, which became known as the Belgian Congo (now called the Democratic Republic of Congo). This franc (1922) was made in Brussels for use in the Congo.

ANTWERP SIEGE COIN
During the Napoleonic Wars, Belgium and the Netherlands were ruled by France. The N on this copper coin stands for Napoleon, whose supporters were besieged in Antwerp in 1814.

Leopold I of Belgium

Willem III of the Netherlands

ROYAL GOLD
After the defeat of Napoleon in 1814, both Belgium and the Netherlands were united as the Kingdom of the United Netherlands. In 1830, Belgium became a separate kingdom. Both kingdoms issued coins with royal portraits.

BELGIAN WAR MONEY
During the First World War, special emergency banknotes were used in occupied Belgium. They could only be changed into the official notes of the National Bank of Belgium three months after the end of the war. This one-franc note was issued in 1917.

Belgium

The Netherlands

BF50 BF20 BF5

Fl5 Fl1 25 cents

TODAY'S MONEY
On January 1, 1999, the euro became the official currency of Belgium and the Netherlands, replacing the Belgian franc and the Dutch guilder. Euro coins and notes circulate starting January 2002.

Italy

THE LIRA WAS ESTABLISHED as Italy's national currency from the mid-19th century when Vittorio Emanuele II became King of Italy. The word lira comes from the Latin word libra, the unit of weight used to set the value of early Roman copper money. Before they used coins, the Romans made payments with cattle and weighed lumps of copper. They got the idea for coins during the third century B.C. from the Greek cities of southern Italy and Sicily where coins had been in use for over 200 years. Early Roman coins were versions of Greek coins or weighed copper money with Greek designs added to them (pp. 10–11). Italian cities such as Pavia, Genoa, Venice, Florence, and Amalfi dominated European trade for centuries. Italian gold ducats were used and imitated throughout Europe and the Eastern Mediterranean countries.

In the time of Augustus, soldiers of the Roman army were paid 225 denarii a year

GREEK SILVER
Many Greek settlements in southern Italy issued coins from the 6th century B.C. This example was minted at Taranto during the 4th century

X, the Roman numeral 10, showed that this silver denarius was worth 10 of the copper one-pound coins

I, the Roman numeral 1, showed that this coin represented one pound (libra) of copper

EARLY ROMAN MONEY
Rome's first money took the form of cast copper lumps, like the one above, weighed out in payments. During the 3rd century, coin-shaped cast copper lumps (left) were used instead (pp. 10–11). A silver coin (denarius), showing the head of the goddess Roma, was issued at the same time

Silver denarius of Julius Caesar, B.C. 44

Gold aureus of Augustus, B.C. 27 – A.D. 14

Bronze sestertius of Nero, A.D. 54–68

ROMAN EMPIRE COINS
Silver, gold, and bronze coins were issued by most Roman emperors. Their portrait was normally the main design. The emperors often used these coins to make themselves known to their subjects. It was a good way to show people what they looked like, what they did, and what their titles were. Remember, there were no newspapers or televisions in those days!

BARBARIAN COIN
You can just see the twin founders of Rome – Romulus and Remus – and the wolf who helped raise them on this bronze coin issued by the Ostrogoth (Barbarian) conquerors of the city in the 6th century.

ANYONE FOR THE GAMES?
The most famous standing monument of the Roman Empire, the Colosseum, was pictured on coins in the year A.D. 80 when it was completed. It was here that the games were held, when men (gladiators) and animals fought to the death to provide entertainment for the bloodthirsty emperors and citizens.

This 20-"ducat" coin is from the "duchy" of Venice

ARABS AND NORMANS
This gold coin was issued by the Arab rulers of Sicily. The crisscross pattern on it is made up of Arabic writing. The copper coin was made by the Norman rulers of Naples who fought the Arabs for control of southern Italy during the late 11th century. The Normans won.

DUCAT AND FLORIN
During the 13th century, the Italian cities of Venice and Florence began to issue gold coins called ducats or sequins in Venice, and florins in Florence. The large coin on the left is a 20-ducat piece from Venice. The smaller piece is a Florentine florin. The first German gold coins were modeled on the florin (p. 32).

PRINCE AND POPE
A revival of Roman Empire coin designs appeared in Italy in the late 15th century; lifelike portraits of rulers were put on the coins. The ruler on the silver coin is Cosimo Medici of Florence (1536–1574), and the gold coin shows Pope Leo X, Medici, (1513–1521). The Medici family gained great wealth as merchants and bankers, and were extremely influential in Florence.

Austrian coin

Sardinian coin

Spanish coin

CONTENDING POWERS
A copper coin of the Austrian Empress, Maria Theresa (1740–1780), a gold coin of Vittorio Amadeo of Savoy, King of Sardinia (1773–1796), and a silver coin of Ferdinand IV, the Spanish king of the Two Sicilies (1759–1825), represent the three main powers struggling for control of Italy during the 18th century.

ROMAN "ASSIGNAT" *right*
In 1798, the states ruled by the Pope rejected his authority and together formed the Roman Republic. Like the French Republic that inspired it, the Roman Republic also issued "assignats" (p. 31).

Year 7 of the French Republic

LIRE NOTE *below*
The lira became the national currency of Italy in 1861 when Vittorio Emanuele II became King of Italy. This 30-lire note was issued in 1884 by a Sardinian bank.

ITALIAN BANKERS
It was in northern Italy, particularly in the area known as Lombardy, that the practice of banking first began during the 14th century. This was the beginning of modern commercial banking as we know it today.

Bimetallic coin

TODAY'S MONEY
Since January 1, 1999, the euro has been the official currency of Italy, replacing the lira. Euro notes and coins come into circulation starting January 1, 2002.

Signatures of bank officials

POLITICAL COIN
This 1923 two-lire coin of King Vittorio Emanuele III used the Fascist emblem (a bundle of sticks and an ax) as its main design. As a protest, an anti-Fascist user of the coin stamped the Communist emblem of a hammer and sickle on it.

SMALL CHANGE
A shortage of small-denomination coins during the 1970s forced shopkeepers to give telephone tokens and candy as change.

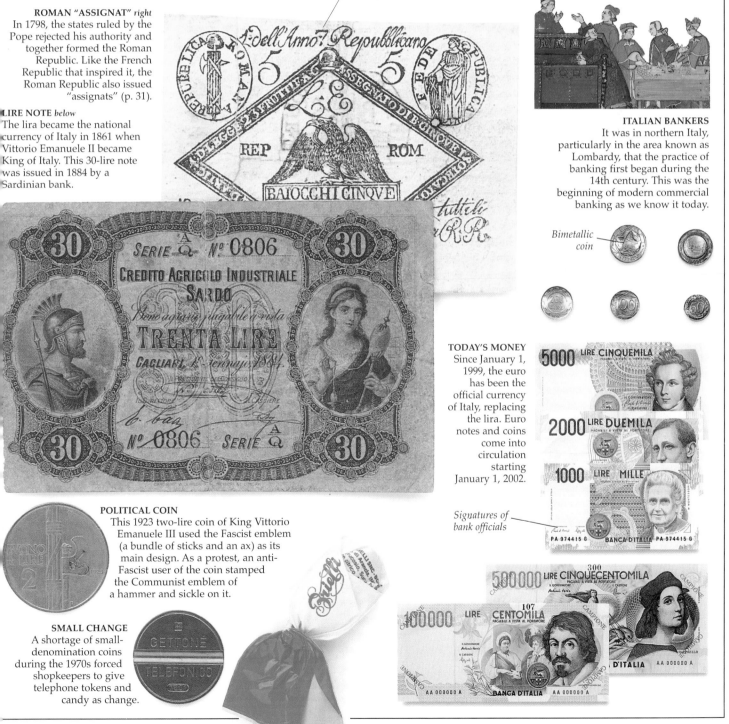

Spain and Portugal

In 1492, CHRISTOPHER COLUMBUS set out from Spain to open up a westward route to the East, and found the Americas. Six years later, Vasco da Gama from Portugal opened the sea route around Africa to India. These two events dramatically changed the history of money. They led to the issue of European-style coins in the Americas, Africa, and eventually Asia, and also brought to Europe vast amounts of gold and silver from those continents. Spain shipped into Europe and Asia millions of silver "pieces of eight" from Mexico, Peru, and Bolivia in South America. Portugal supplied Europe with gold taken from Africa, India, China, and Brazil. Spain's peseta, introduced in 1869, got its name from the popular term for a small silver coin. The modern Portuguese escudo is a more recent creation; it was first issued in 1915.

Spanish and Portuguese galleons were often loaded with treasure

Greek coin from Emporium, B.C. 250

Carthaginian coin, Spain, B.C. 210

Spanish Celtic coin, c. B.C. 100

Coin of Carthaginian settlement at Salacia in Portugal, c. B.C. 100

ANCIENT COINS
Greek colonists had introduced coinage into Spain and Portugal by the 4th century B.C. Their main mint was at Emporium (now called Ampurias) in northeast Spain. Later, Carthaginian, Celtic, and Roman coins were also issued.

Spanish Roman copper coin from Saragossa, c. A.D. 20

Moorish gold coin

Visigoth gold coin

Coin from Castile, copying a Moorish design

Portuguese gold coin

MOORISH GOLD
In 711, an Arab-led Moorish army conquered the Visigoths in Spain and began to issue their own coins. The Islamic designs on Moorish coins were copied on the earliest coins of the Christian kings of Castile and Portugal, who had driven the Moors out of Spain by the 15th century.

Roman aqueduct of Segovia, the mark of the Segovian mint

NEW WORLDS
The search for gold took Columbus to the Americas, and Vasco da Gama to India. The gold they found was used to make coins like the piece (top left) of Ferdinand and Isabella of Spain (1479–1504), and the piece (top right) of John III of Portugal (1521–1557).

Silver "pieces of eight"

Robinson Crusoe

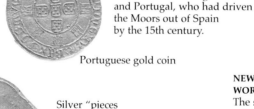

Gold doubloon

SPANISH EMPIRE
The Spanish conquerors of the Americas were quick to exploit the rich gold sources and silver mines they found in Mexico, Bolivia, and Peru. These crudely made coins, silver "pieces of eight" and gold doubloons, were loaded on to treasure ships bound for Europe. These ships often fell prey to pirates!

"I got all my cargo on shore . . . I found there were three great bags of pieces of eight . . . and in one of them, wrapped up in paper, six doubloons of gold."

PORTUGUESE EMPIRE
Portugal's empire in the Indian Ocean was based on trade. The tin coin (left) was made in 1511 for local use at the port of Malacca in Malaya. In 1693, gold was discovered in Brazil, and was made into coins like the 1725 Portuguese coin (right) in Rio de Janeiro, Brazil. The coins were then exported.

CONQUISTADORS VERSUS INDIANS
Spanish conquistadors fought the Inca and Aztec peoples of the Americas for their supplies of gold and silver.

50-reales coin made in Segovia from Spanish American silver

Original VIII (eight) stamp

MONEY TROUBLES
The flow of silver and gold into Spain made it the richest country in the world, but it wasted the money on war. Prices went up and copper coins had to be revalued. This copper coin was revalued from eight maravedis to 12 maravedis in 1652.

XII (twelve) stamp revaluing coin

Ferdinand VII

Joseph Napoleon

Duke of Wellington

TWO SPANISH KINGS
In 1808, there were two new kings crowned in Spain: the legitimate heir, Ferdinand VII, and Napoleon's brother, Joseph. A British army, led by the future Duke of Wellington, drove the French usurper out. Both kings issued their own coins, but the British army used its own money, including tokens showing Wellington's portrait.

PORTUGUESE WAR NOTE
After the Napoleonic War, civil war continued in Portugal. This 1805 note was reissued in 1828 by the usurper, Miguel I.

SPANISH CIVIL WAR
This note was issued by the Spanish Republican government during the Civil War (1936–1939). After the War, coins were issued showing the portrait of General Franco, victorious commander of the anti-Republican forces.

"LIBERTY AND DEMOCRACY"
These words are inscribed on this Portuguese coin celebrating the restoration of democratic government in 1974.

Spain

Pta 50   Pta 100   Pta 25   Pta 5

Ferdinand and Isabella were patrons of Christopher Columbus

Portugal

Esc 200   Esc 100   Esc 50   Esc 20

TODAY'S MONEY
On January 1, 1999, the euro replaced the peseta in Spain and the escudo in Portugal. Euro notes and coins circulate starting 2002.

Greece and Turkey

TODAY'S COINS ALL HAVE THEIR ORIGIN in the Ancient Greek versions of the coins first made in Ancient Turkey (pp. 10–11). The Ancient Greeks gave coins their distinctive round shape with designs on both sides. Since then, Greece and Turkey have had many different rulers – Greek, Persian, Roman, Byzantine, Turkish, French, Italian, British, Russian, and German – who have all issued coins of their own. The current money of both countries, the Greek drachma and the Turkish lira, are of quite recent origin. The drachma, which takes its name from a coin of Ancient Greece, began in 1831 when Greece became independent. The lira, first issued as paper money in 1930, represented the renaming of the Turkish pound (livre).

"AS RICH AS CROESUS"
This saying refers to the wealth of Croesus, King of Lydia (c. B.C. 560–547). He is thought to have issued the coin above, one of the first gold coins in the world.

ROYAL IMAGES
Greek kings are to be seen on these two silver coins; Philip II of Macedonia (B.C. 359–336) on horseback (above), and Antiochus I of Syria (B.C. 281–261) on a coin from southern Turkey (right).

FLYING PIG
The design and inscription on this silver coin identify it as a 5th-century B.C. issue of the city of Ialysus on the Greek island of Rhodes.

Greek writing was used in the Byzantine Empire

BYZANTINE GOLD
The Byzantine emperor, Alexius II (1297–1330), issued coins like this one in Constantinople (now Istanbul), Turkey and Thessalonika, Greece.

Coin issued for Mark Antony before the battle of Actium (B.C. 31)

SULEIMAN THE MAGNIFICENT
Suleiman, the most powerful of all the Ottoman sultans (1494–1566) issued the gold coin below. His reign was noted for its military power.

Seated warrior is holding a severed head

ROMAN COINS
The Romans issued many coins in the parts of their empire now known as Greece and Turkey. The gold coin (above right) is a Greek issue for Mark Antony. The large bronze coin from Turkey features the Roman Emperor, Caracalla.

THE CRUSADES
The small silver coin (top) was issued by a French crusader who ruled as the Duke of Athens (1280–1287). The copper coins were made by rival forces fighting for eastern Turkey. The lion's face coin (center) was issued by the Christian Armenian kings of Cilicia (1187–1218), and the seated warrior coin (bottom) by the Turkish rulers of Mardin.

Silver aqche of Thessalonika (Salonika), 1574

Paper kurus of the Ottoman Imperial Bank, 1877

Gold altin of Istanbul, 1520

Tughra emblem

Silver kurus of Istanbul, 1769

THE SULTAN'S MONEY
The Turkish Ottoman sultans ruled both Greece and Turkey. They issued their pictureless coins throughout their empire, which stretched from Algeria to Iraq, and from Hungary to Yemen. The knotted emblem (known as a tughra) on the large silver coin and the note is the official "signature" of the sultans.

40

Venetian copper soldo of the 18th century

COINS OF CORFU
Corfu and the other Ionian islands were for a long time the only parts of Greece to escape Turkish Ottoman rule. From 1402 until 1797 they were ruled by Venice, but they then passed briefly through the hands of France, Russia, Turkey, and France again until 1815, when Britain took control. In 1863, they finally became part of Greece.

Russian copper gazetta, 1801

British copper obol, 1819

The phoenix, symbol of rebirth, taken from a Greek banknote

Otto I gold coin

INDEPENDENT GREECE
In 1828, Greece, the "mother of democracy," achieved independence from Turkish rule. The first coins, like this copper 10-lepton of 1831, were issued by the Greek Republic. In 1831, Greece became a kingdom under Otto I of Bavaria, whose portrait appears on the gold 20-drachma coin.

Greek Republic copper coin

CORFU CRICKET
During the British occupation of Corfu, the British troops missed their traditional game of cricket, so they built a cricket field in Corfu town The venerable game of cricket is still played there regularly, but by the Greeks, not the British.

National Bank of Greece one-drachma note, 1885

ISLAND MONEY
The Greek island of Thasos remained under Turkish rule until 1914. This Turkish copper 40-para coin was countermarked by the Greek community in Thasos in 1893.

NEW COINS, OLD DESIGNS
The second Greek Republic (1925–1935) used Ancient Greek coin designs on its new issues. The design of this two-drachma coin is the head of Athena, copied from an ancient coin of Corinth.

Turkey

TL 50,000

TL 25,000

TL 10,000

TURKISH REPUBLIC
In 1923, Ottoman rule in Turkey ceased, and it became a republic under the leadership of Kamel Ataturk. His portrait appears on this 100-kurus (one-lira) coin, which was issued in 1934.

TODAY'S MONEY: TURKEY
The Turkish lira (pound) is divided into 100 kurus (piastre), but kurus coins are no longer issued.

Greece

Dr100   Dr50   Dr20   Dr5

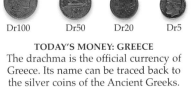

TODAY'S MONEY: GREECE
The drachma is the official currency of Greece. Its name can be traced back to the silver coins of the Ancient Greeks.

LOCAL GREEK NOTE
During the World War II, many locally issued notes were in use. This 5000-drachma note is from Zagora.

Denmark and Norway

Coin of King Cnut (1019–1035) from his mint at Lund

Norwegian penny of Viking King Olaf Kyrre (1067–1093)

SILVER PENNIES
English designs were copied on early Danish and Norwegian silver pennies. An example of the Norwegian coin above was recently found at a Viking settlement in North America.

B̲efore D̲enmark and N̲orway had their own coins, the Vikings introduced French, German, English, and Islamic coins that they had captured as loot or acquired in trade. During the 10th and 11th centuries, the Danish and Norwegian kings began to issue their own coins, with designs copied from English silver pennies. Today, Denmark and Norway both use the krone, divided into 100 øre, as their currency. The same denominations are used in Sweden (pp. 44–45). These three separate currencies were introduced in 1873 as part of a common Scandinavian system. The krone ("crown") had originally been a silver coin with a crown design issued by the kings of Denmark and Norway in the 17th and 18th centuries. The øre was of Swedish origin.

CNUT RULES THE WAVES!
According to legend, King Cnut of Denmark and England tried to prove his power by commanding the tide to stop; he failed. Cnut issued English-style pennies for use in both kingdoms.

KING OF DENMARK AND NORWAY
King Christian IV (1588–1648) was king of both Denmark and Norway, but he issued separate coins for each kingdom. The silver coin on the left is Danish, and the one on the right, Norwegian.

The letter "C" is the initial of the king who issued this klippe, Christian V

ROYAL GIFTS
Square coins, called klippe, were often issued in Denmark during the 16th and 17th centuries. Square coins were first used as emergency issues in war, as they were quicker to make than round ones. These two klippe are special coins that were made for the king to give away as presents.

Pillars and globe design copied from a "piece of eight" (p. 21)

The Lapp reindeer herders of northern Norway used reindeer and furs as payments

TRADE COINS
This silver coin, copied from a Spanish American "piece of eight," was made in 1777 for the Danish Asiatic Society to use in China. The picture on the small gold coin (1726) shows Christiansborg, a Danish settlement in West Africa where the gold used for the coin came from.

A Viking warship

MARKS AND SKILLINGS
During the 18th century, the Danish and Norwegian monetary system was based on the mark, which was divided into 16 skillings. This silver krone of 1723 was worth four marks. 64 of the copper skillings (far right) made a krone.

The lion with ax design was used on Norwegian coins. There are four on these pages

PAPER AND SILVER DALERS

In 1813, the Danish government introduced a currency based on a daler of 96 skilling. This daler note was issued in Christiania (the old name for Oslo, Norway) by the Danish Royal Bank of Copenhagen. The daler continued to be used in Norway after it came under the control of the King of Sweden in 1814. This silver daler was issued in 1823.

Dolphin and grain symbolize fishing and agriculture

SCANDINAVIAN MONEY

In 1873, a unified currency system was created for Denmark, Norway, and Sweden. The same denominations were issued by each country, but different designs were used. The 20-kroner and 5-øre coins above are from Denmark (top) and Norway (bottom). For Sweden's versions, see p. 45.

EMERGENCY COINS

During World War II, there was a shortage of copper, because it was used to make shell cases. This meant that both Denmark and Norway had to use different metals to make their coins. Norway issued coins made of iron (left), and Denmark issued coins made from aluminum (right) and zinc.

PAPER KRONE

During World War I, and for a few years after, local emergency paper money was issued in Denmark. This example was made by the Odense Credit Bank.

ODENSE KREDITBANK

1 KRONE 1

TODAY'S MONEY

Denmark and Norway both use the same currency names. The krone, which is divided into 100 øre, was adopted by both countries in 1873.

Norway

NKr 10   NKr 1   50 øre

Denmark

DKr 1   25 øre   1 øre

Sweden and Finland

As well as issuing Europe's first paper money, Sweden issued the biggest coins ever made – copper plate money. These huge rectangular coins could weigh up to about 42 lb (19 kg)! Today, Sweden's money is not so strange; it is based on the krona, divided into 100 öre. Until 1809, Finland used Swedish money since it was ruled by the Swedish crown. However, in that year Finland came under Russian control, and the rouble and kopek were used. Later the markka and penni were also introduced by the Russians.

SWEDISH COPIES
The coin (left) is a copy of an Islamic coin. The penny (right) was made by visiting English coinmakers.

ONE-SIDED COINS
Silver pennies with a design on one side only were made in the 13th century. The M (top) is for King Magnus of Sweden; the A (right) is for Abo, the old name for the Finnish city, Turku.

DALERS, DUCATS, AND ÖRE
In 1534, Gustav I Vasa (1523–1560) introduced Sweden's first silver daler (left). This also circulated in Finland, part of his kingdom. Gustav II Adolf (1611–1632) introduced Sweden's first copper coinage, square pieces denominated in öre (center). Swedish rule extended into Germany, and Gustav Adolf II issued gold ducats for his subjects there. His daughter, Kristina (1634–1654), is shown on the silver daler (right).

Massive man-powered drop hammers were used to stamp the designs onto plate money

PLATE MONEY
Sweden first issued huge copper coins called plate money during Kristina's reign. There were rich copper mines at Avesta and Falun (the copper mountain at Falun is shown on the token above). Plate money was very heavy; the square one-daler piece (right) weighs almost 4 lb (2 kg), so paper money, like this check worth 288 dalers, was used instead.

Anno 1717.
Ein Daler Silfwermynt

Flagermarck

Job. Ekendall

DALER TOKENS
In 1717, the Swedish government ran out of money because of a costly war with Russia. It issued both paper and small copper dalers instead of the plate money. The copper dalers were decorated with pictures of Roman gods. The dalers here show Mercury, Jupiter, Saturn, and Mars.

Paper daler

Copper dalers

Notes were only valid if all three signatures appeared

Russian Imperial two-headed eagle

ÅR 1840 **N° 76141**

Tjugu Kopek

UTE STORFURSTENDÓMET FINLANDS WÄXEL - DEPOSITIONS - OCH LÅNE - BANK ÅR. INSATT EN SUMMA AF TJUGU KOPEK KEISERLIGA RYSKA BANKO - ASSIGNATIONER. HVILKA 20 KOPEK INNEHAFVAREN HÄRAF HAR ATT ÅTERBEKOMMA.

ДВАДЦАТЬ КОПЬЕКЪ.

Kaxi Kymmendä Kopekaa.

20 KOP

This design is taken from a Finnish banknote; the name of the Bank of Finland is written in Swedish, Finnish, and Russian.

RUSSIAN FINLAND
In 1809, Sweden lost control of Finland to Russia. The Russians introduced into Finland their own roubles and kopeks. The 20-kopek note (right) was issued in 1840. Finland was given its own currency in 1864, when coins denominated in markkaa, divided into 100 penniä, were introduced. The gold coin (above right) is a 20-markkaa piece, and the copper coin below it, a 10-penniä.

COMMON COINS
Sweden's money has been denominated in kronor and öre since 1873 when, along with Denmark and Norway, it reorganized its currency to form a common system. The öre was already in use in Sweden. This 5-öre coin was issued in 1857, but the gold 20-kronor was issued in 1876.

Finland

Fmk 10

Fmk 2

Fmk 1

INDEPENDENT FINLAND
Finland had a different coinage system from the other Scandinavian countries. When the country became independent in 1917, it kept the currency system introduced by the Russians.

Sweden

50 FEMTIO KRONOR

100

500 FEM HUNDRA KRONOR

SPECIMEN

SKr 5 SKr 1 50 öre

TODAY'S MONEY
Since January 1, 1999, the euro has been the official currency of Finland. Euro notes and coins circulate starting 2002. The official currency of Sweden is based on the krona, which is divided into 100 öre.

The Royal Mint was located in or near the Tower of London for almost 1,000 years

United Kingdom

ALL OF THE REGIONS of the United Kingdom of Great Britain – England, Scotland, Northern Ireland, Wales, the Isle of Man, and the Channel Isles – now use a monetary system based on the pound sterling (£) divided into 100 pennies. Before 1971, the pound sterling was divided into 240 pennies, 12 of which made a shilling. Different forms of paper money circulate in each region, except England and Wales, which share Bank of England notes. Different coins are issued for the Isle of Man and the Channel Islands of Guernsey and Jersey. The other regions use British coins made by the Royal Mint in Wales. Celts and Romans introduced coins into Britain, and Britain has since been responsible for introducing its own money to many parts of the world, largely through trade and war. The pound sterling is still one of the world's most important currencies.

CELTIC GOLD
This Celtic coin (c. A.D. 10–40) names a famous Ancient British king, Cunobelin, king of the Catuvellauni tribe.

ROMAN MINT
The Roman mint at London (Londinium) made this bronze coin for the Emperor Maximian. The name of the mint, "LON," is at the bottom of the coin.

SAXON AND VIKING PENNIES
The Anglo-Saxons introduced the silver penny; the coin (left) shows the Saxon king Alfred the Great. The coin (right) names Eric Bloodaxe, the Viking King of York.

Silver sixpence

MACHINE-MADE MONEY
The silver sixpence of Elizabeth I (above) was the first to be made in 1566 with a screw-press coining machine like the one in the picture at the Tower mint (above left)

Scottish kings always faced to the side on sterling pennies

Punch marks to test that coin was solid gold (p. 19)

STERLING SILVER PENNIES
King Edward I introduced a new silver penny, the "sterling," in 1279. His new coins were so frequently used in trade that many foreign copies were made of them. These coins are sterlings of Edward I (left) and Robert Bruce, King of Scotland (right).

GROAT AND NOBLE
As trade expanded during the 14th century, the standard silver penny was joined by several new, more valuable coins. The silver groat (left) was worth four pennies, and the gold noble (right), 80 pennies.

18TH-CENTURY SMALL CHANGE
Local small change reappeared in the late 18th century when the government failed to issue copper coins. Local traders responded by issuing their own copper tokens. The Welsh druid halfpenny (top) was made by a Welsh copper mining company; the Lady Godiva coin (center) was issued in Coventry.

"The Queen's Head" public house, London

SMALL CHANGE
During the 17th century, a shortage of small change prompted traders and innkeepers to issue brass farthings (quarter penny) and halfpennies.

COPPER HALFPENNY
Britain's first official copper halfpenny of 1672 had the image of Britannia on the back.

LADY GODIVA
According to legend, Lady Godiva rode naked through the streets of Coventry to persuade her husband to lower the heavy taxes. The only person to peek at her as she rode became known as "Peeping Tom."

The thick rim of the 1797 steam press coins earned them the nickname "cartwheel"

GOLD SOVEREIGN
The first British pound coin (worth 240 silver pennies) was introduced by King Henry VII in 1489. This example (c. 1545) was struck at the Southwark mint for King Henry VIII, whose large figure is seen seated on the throne.

GOLD UNITE
A new pound coin was introduced by King James I in 1604. This one (1650) was made during the English Civil War when England was ruled by Parliament after James' son, King Charles I, had been executed.

GOLD "GUINEA"
This machine-made gold pound (1663) depicts King Charles II. The elephant at the bottom shows that it was made with gold from Africa's Guinea Coast.

GOLD SOVEREIGN
A new gold pound coin was issued during King George III's reign (1738–1820). It was called a sovereign, like the first gold pound coin.

PAPER GUINEA
Paper money (pp. 12–13) became popular in Britain during the 18th century. This Scottish guinea note of 1777 was the first to be printed in three colors.

£2   £1   50p   20p

10p   5p   2p   1p

Queen Victoria liked to give 5 pound coins like this one as a souvenir to her court visitors.

The 1849 florin

DECIMAL COINS
The first attempt at decimalization (division into units of 10) was made in 1849 with the introduction of a two-shilling coin, the florin, which was a tenth of a pound. This became a ten-pence coin after full decimalization in 1971.

1971 equivalent ten-pence coin

TODAY'S MONEY
The United Kingdom has a national currency based on the pound sterling, divided into 100 pennies. Some parts of the country are permitted to use their own local coins and banknotes.

£1 Jersey   5p Isle of Man   2p Guernsey

WARTIME SIXPENCE NOTE
The Island of Jersey issued its own locally designed and printed notes during World War II.

Scotland

Northern Ireland

United States of America

THE CURRENCY OF THE UNITED STATES of America is made up of dollars and cents. Coins and paper money were first introduced into North America by various European settlers. But Britain did not issue coins or notes for its settlers, so they used tobacco, shell beads, (pp. 8–9), and imported Spanish "pieces of eight" (known as "dollars") instead. The colonists also issued their own paper money. The dollar had already been chosen as the currency of the United States of America before the Declaration of Independence was signed on July 4, l776. The first US dollars were paper – the Continental Currency bills issued from 1775; silver dollars were also issued from 1794. The US dollar, made of paper again since 1862, is the world's most widely used currency.

The American bald eagle

BRITISH COLONIAL MONEY
The British colonists did not have any British coins. Instead, they used beads and tobacco, and made their own coins and paper money. This was denominated in pounds, shillings, and pence like these Massachusetts shillings of 1652, and Pennsylvanian four-pence note of 1755.

FIRST COINS OF THE UNITED STATES
After a period of planning and experiment, the United States began in 1793 to issue a regular coinage based on the dollar. The 1793 copper cent (top right) was followed by the silver dollar in 1794 (top center), and the gold 10-dollar "eagle" in 1795 (top left). The size of the cent was based on the British halfpenny, and the dollar on the Spanish "piece of eight."

Chain on this tin pattern represents the 13 states united against Britain

CONTINENTAL CURRENCY
When the colonists broke with Britain, they financed their Revolutionary War with paper dollars issued by the Continental Congress. In 1776, a silver dollar was planned, but not introduced, although tin patterns for it exist.

LEAF MONEY
Tobacco leaves were made into bundles and officially used as money in Virginia and Maryland in the 17th and 18th centuries.

ENTER WHO DARES!
Fort Knox in Kentucky has been the site of the United States Gold Bullion Depository since 1938. The gold is stored in concrete and steel vaults inside a bomb-proof building that is protected by guards armed with machine guns.

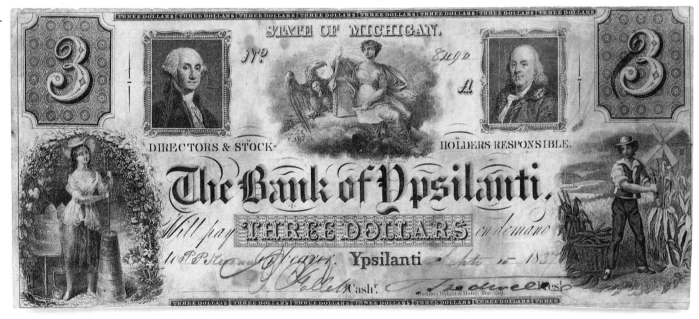

THREE-DOLLAR BILL
During the 19th century, most of the money used in the United States was in the form of paper dollars. This note was issued in 1837 by a small private bank in Ypsilanti, Michigan.

DEPRESSION BREADLINE
After the Wall Street Crash of 1929, the value of the dollar fell drastically. By the end of 1931, 4,000 banks had closed. There was massive unemployment, and many people had to rely on charity to eat, lining up for regular food handouts.

GOLD RUSH!
After the discovery of gold in California in 1848, gold dust and nuggets were used as money in the mining camps. When the gold reached San Francisco, the center of the gold-mining area, it was made into coins like this 50-dollar piece made in 1852.

Seal of the Department of the Treasury

EISENHOWER DOLLAR
Recent coins have a presidential portrait as their main design: Eisenhower on the dollar (right); Kennedy on the half-dollar; Washington on the quarter; Franklin D. Roosevelt on the dime; Jefferson on the nickel; and Lincoln on the cent.

BICENTENNIAL QUARTER
For the celebrations of the 200th anniversary of American Independence in 1976, commemorative coins like this one were issued.

FAILED DOLLAR
In 1979, a dollar coin portraying the feminist leader Susan B. Anthony was issued. It was not popular, and was withdrawn from use. There are now 441 million Susan B. Anthony dollars under lock and key, awaiting their fate!

LAS VEGAS
Dollar coins still survive in the casinos of Las Vegas and Atlantic City, New Jersey, where they are poured into the slots of "one-armed bandit" gambling machines.

| 25 cents "quarter" | 10 cents "dime" | 5 cents "nickel" | 1 cents "penny" |

TODAY'S MONEY
US currency is based on the dollar, divided into 100 cents. Each coin has its own nickname, and US bills are popularly known as "greenbacks," because of the color of the ink on their backs.

Canada

Coins and banknotes were first introduced into Canada by British and French settlers, but the native peoples continued to use their own traditional means of payment, such as beads and blankets. The settlers preferred to use furs and grain as money, or to make their own! The dollar and cent currency used today was introduced during the 1850s. Forms of the British and French currency systems were in use before that but, as in the USA, the Spanish dollar was the main coin in circulation. The Dominion of Canada, established in 1867, adopted the dollar as its official currency in 1868.

FRENCH CANADIAN COIN
Canada's first coins were made in Paris for French settlers on the orders of Louis XIV of France. This silver piece was made in 1670.

"BEAVER" MONEY
The Hudson Bay (Trading) Company issued its own paper money like this one-shilling note, but the traders used beaver skins as money. It also issued this brass token for one beaver skin.

Nº 3214 ONE SHILLING Sterlg 1845.
Hudsons Bay Company.
Promise to pay the Bearer on Demand the Sum of ONE SHILLING for the YORK FACTORY, in RUPERTS LAND in a Bill of Exchange payable Sixty days after Sight at the Hudsons Bay House, London. 3214
LONDON, the 1st day of May 1845. For the Governor & Company of Adventurers of England, trading into Hudsons Bay
Nº 3214 A Burlay SECRETARY.
Issued at York Factory, the 4th day of March 1846 by
GOVERNOR.
Ent. John Black Accountant.

PROVINCIAL TOKENS
British sterling was the official money of Canada until the 1850s, but most provinces had established their own currency systems based on the Spanish and American dollars. Local tokens were made for small change. In the English-speaking provinces, they were pennies and halfpennies. In French-speaking Quebec (Lower Canada), the tokens were denominated in sou.

Nova Scotia
penny token, 1824

Upper Canada
halfpenny token, 1833

Lower Canada
sou token, 1837

Lower Canada
two-sou token, 1837

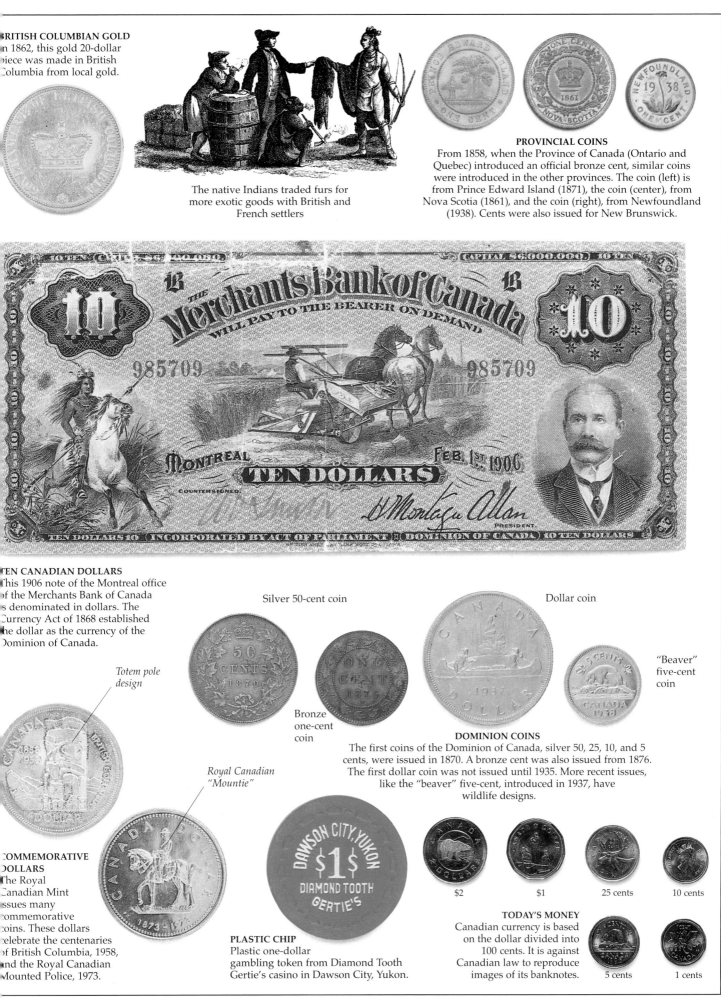

BRITISH COLUMBIAN GOLD
In 1862, this gold 20-dollar piece was made in British Columbia from local gold.

The native Indians traded furs for more exotic goods with British and French settlers

PROVINCIAL COINS
From 1858, when the Province of Canada (Ontario and Quebec) introduced an official bronze cent, similar coins were introduced in the other provinces. The coin (left) is from Prince Edward Island (1871), the coin (center), from Nova Scotia (1861), and the coin (right), from Newfoundland (1938). Cents were also issued for New Brunswick.

TEN CANADIAN DOLLARS
This 1906 note of the Montreal office of the Merchants Bank of Canada is denominated in dollars. The Currency Act of 1868 established the dollar as the currency of the Dominion of Canada.

Totem pole design

Silver 50-cent coin

Dollar coin

"Beaver" five-cent coin

Bronze one-cent coin

DOMINION COINS
The first coins of the Dominion of Canada, silver 50, 25, 10, and 5 cents, were issued in 1870. A bronze cent was also issued from 1876. The first dollar coin was not issued until 1935. More recent issues, like the "beaver" five-cent, introduced in 1937, have wildlife designs.

Royal Canadian "Mountie"

COMMEMORATIVE DOLLARS
The Royal Canadian Mint issues many commemorative coins. These dollars celebrate the centenaries of British Columbia, 1958, and the Royal Canadian Mounted Police, 1973.

PLASTIC CHIP
Plastic one-dollar gambling token from Diamond Tooth Gertie's casino in Dawson City, Yukon.

$2 $1   25 cents   10 cents

TODAY'S MONEY
Canadian currency is based on the dollar divided into 100 cents. It is against Canadian law to reproduce images of its banknotes.

5 cents   1 cents

Australia and New Zealand

BRITISH POUNDS, SHILLINGS, AND PENCE arrived in Australia and New Zealand with the first British settlers, but because of the many trade ships that went there, Indian, Dutch, Spanish, and Portuguese coins were more common. In 1792, settlers at Sydney Cove found a form of money more to their taste when *The Hope*, an American merchantship, delivered a cargo of rum. This precious liquid circulated as money in New South Wales until it was replaced in 1813 by Spanish American silver dollars (p. 21), which circulated officially until 1829. Today's dollar currencies were introduced by Australia in 1966, and New Zealand in 1967, when both countries adopted a decimal currency system in place of pounds, shillings, and pence.

GOLD!
In 1851, gold was found in Australia. Gold dust was used as money until 1852 when ingots (above) were made in Adelaide, followed by coins (top right). Unofficial "Kangaroo Office" gold coins (center) were made in 1853 at Port Phillip, Melbourne. A mint was established in Sydney in 1853 to make sovereigns (right) and half-sovereigns.

"HOLEY DOLLAR" AND "DUMP"
From 1813 until 1822, dollars with a hole were the official currency of New South Wales. The silver "dump" cut from the middle was also official money. The dollar was valued at five shillings, and the dump at 15 pence.

THE GREAT GOLD RUSH
The discovery of gold in Australia prompted many prospectors to search for it.

No. 3142 No. 3142

Wellington, New Zealand 1st Jan.y 1857.

THE ORIENTAL BANK CORPORATION
Promise to pay the Bearer on demand at their Office here ONE POUND *for value received.*

By order of the Court of Directors.

Account.ᵗ Manager.

Thames Goldfields penny token 1874

"Advance New Zealand" penny token, 1881

NEW ZEALAND NOTES AND TOKENS
Although British coins were the official currency of New Zealand, most of the money in use during the 19th century was locally issued copper tokens, and notes like this one issued in 1857 by a British commercial bank. More than 140 different tokens like those above were also issued.

BANK of QUEENSLAND, LIMITED.

TOOWOOMBA

THREE   THREE

№ 1725   № 1725

I Promise to pay the Bearer on Demand the Sum of THREE POUNDS in Cash here 2nd Jany 1865. Brisbane 2nd Jany 1865.

Batho & Co London.

THREE

FOR THE BANK of QUEENSLAND, LIMITED.

Ent William Anderson ACC.T   A Anderson MANAGER.

BRISBANE.

Australia's flightless, swift-running bird, the emu

BARTER
When Europeans arrived in Australia and New Zealand, they swapped cloth and metal tools for food with the Aboriginal and Maori peoples.

AUSTRALIAN NOTES AND TOKENS
During the second half of the 19th century, banknotes and local trade tokens provided most of the money in Australia. The Bank of Queensland issued the three-pound note (above) from its Brisbane office in 1865. The copper tokens from Tasmania and Western Australia were struck in Melbourne.

AUSTRALIAN COINS
In 1910, the Australians minted their own Australian Commonwealth coins. Shillings (left), silver florins (top), sixpences, and threepences were issued. From 1911, bronze pennies (right) and halfpennies joined them.

NEW ZEALAND COINS
In 1933, New Zealanders also got their own coins. Silver half-crowns, florins (left), shillings (bottom left), sixpences, and threepences were issued. Bronze pennies and halfpennies (below) were made from 1940.

This Maori "good luck" image (tiki) was shown on the bronze half-penny from 1940 until 1965.

New Zealand

NZ$2
NZ$1
20 cents

TODAY'S MONEY
Both Australia and New Zealand base their currencies on a dollar divided into 100 cents. Australia's banknotes are made of plastic and have a transparent window.

Transparent window is a security device

A$2
A$1
50 cents

Australia

53

China and Japan

THE MODERN CURRENCIES of both China and Japan developed from silver dollars (p. 21) introduced by European and American traders. They were exchanged for silk, tea, gold bars, porcelain, and rhubarb! The dollars – called "round coins,"or "yuan" in Chinese and "yen" in Japanese – took over from traditional currencies as the main form of money. China's coinage began in the 6th century B.C. (p. 11), and was later adopted by Japan. In China, silver and gold were used as money only in weighed amounts. The Japanese made coins from the precious metals. Both countries played an important part in the development of paper money (pp. 12–13).

The Great Wall of China stretches for 1,500 miles (2,400 km).

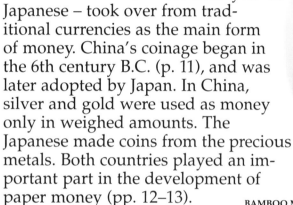

A Chinese money-changer

ANCIENT CHINA
Early Chinese coins were made of cast bronze in the shape of tools, like this hoe-shaped coin (left), c. 300 B.C. This shape was inconvenient, so in 221 B.C. the first emperor of China, Qin Shihuangdi, replaced them with round coins with square holes (below). Tool-shaped coins, like this knife-shaped coin (right), were briefly re-issued by emperor Wang Mang (A.D. 7–23).

Inscription gives weight of coin: half an ounce

THE SHOGUN'S COIN
In 1626, the shogun of Japan introduced new standard bronze coins. The inscription on them meant "generous, ever-lasting money."

BAMBOO MONEY
In 19th-century Shanghai, China, bamboo sticks were used as money instead of the heavy standard coins. This stick was worth 100 coins.

Holes for threading coins on strings

STANDARD COINS
In A.D. 621, the Chinese Tang Dynasty introduced a new standard bronze coin (top left) with a four-character inscription around its square hole. This design was used in China until the last issue in 1912. In A.D. 708, the same type of coin was introduced into Japan (left).

Inscription gives the weight (10 ounces) and the Mint Master's signature

MULTIPLE COIN
During a copper shortage in China, due to the capture of copper-mining areas by rebel forces, "multiple" coins were issued. This one (1854) was worth 1,000 standard coins.

"BIG PIECE" GOLD
This 1860 oban ("big piece") is typical of the gold coins of Japan during the Tokugawa Shogunate (1603–1868). Some Japanese clans issued their own coins, like this lead coin (above) from Kanragori.

The figure on this Taiwan dollar is the Chinese god of long life

PAPER DRAGONS
As well as the silver dollars, the Chinese also used banknotes valued in dollars. This note was issued by the Imperial Bank of Jiangsu Province in 1906.

CHINESE DOLLARS
Many silver dollars were imported into China. In the 19th century, the Chinese began to make their own; first, unofficial local versions like this Taiwan dollar (1840s), then, from 1890, the Imperial Dragon dollars.

MEIJI EMPEROR
The Meiji Emperor, Mutsuhito, reigned in Japan from 1868–1912.

JAPANESE DOLLAR
The dollar influenced Japan to adopt this denomination for its own coinage. In 1870, the Meiji Emperor replaced the traditional Shogun coins with his own "dragon" dollar.

WORKERS OF THE WORLD UNITE!
So reads the slogan on this Chinese dollar issued by the Communist army in northwest China in 1934.

YUAN AND FEN
The Chinese called their dollar "yuan" (the round coin), and their cent "fen" (meaning a hundredth part). This two-fen note was issued by the Chinese People's Bank in 1953.

YEN AND SEN
The Japanese called their dollar "yen" (the round coin), and their cent, "sen" (the name of the traditional standard bronze coin). This ten-sen note of the Meiji Emperor was issued in 1872.

China

Japan

500 yen   10 yen   5 yen

1 yuan   5 jiao   1 jiao

TODAY'S MONEY
Japan's yen and China's yuan both derive their name from the silver dollars issued in both countries in the 19th century. The yuan is divided into 10 jiao or 100 fen.

Africa

SOME OF THE EARLIEST RECORDS of the use of money come from Africa (pp. 8–9). The first African coins were issued about B.C. 500 by a Greek colony on the Libyan coast. Coinage soon became widespread from Egypt to Morocco, as Phoenician, local African, Roman, and Byzantine mints were established. From the 8th century onward, Arab and Berber traders established caravan routes across the Sahara Desert to bring West African gold to the Islamic mints of North Africa, from where it was shipped into Europe to make coins. Farther south, traditional means of payment, such as cattle, salt, cloth, and tools (pp. 8–9), were still the only form of money until coins and banknotes were introduced by European traders and settlers. In some areas, the traditional currencies have survived into the present century.

North

The emblem of Carthage was a horse, shown here as Pegasus

Arabic writing

BERBER GOLD
The Muwahhid Berber rulers of Morocco brought West African gold north across the Sahara. This Muwahhid coin was made in the 13th century.

CARTHAGE
This large silver coin was made to pay troops during Carthage's (an ancient city in Tunisia) war with Rome (B.C. 264–241). The inscription is in Phoenician.

FRENCH MOROCCO
This two-franc note was issued for use in the French Protectorate of Morocco during World War II. The French monetary system was used in Morocco from 1910 until 1960.

KISSI PENNY
Until the 1930s, pieces of iron wire, flattened at both ends, were used as money in Liberia and the neighboring West African states. They were named after the Kissi people who made them.

West

PORTUGUESE AFRICA
This copper macuta was issued in Lisbon in 1762 for use in Angola. "Macuta" was the name of the local copper-bar money.

The Nigerian Ibo people preferred to use copper rings as money (p. 9)

LION DOLLAR
The British colony of Sierra Leone was established as a home for freed African slaves. A coinage of silver dollars was made for Sierra Leone in 1791.

LIBERIA
Liberia was also established as a home for freed slaves. Its American founders issued copper cents for the settlement in 1833. The design shows an African greeting freed slaves arriving home.

INDEPENDENCE
The Gold Coast was the first British colony to achieve independence; it became the new nation of Ghana in 1956. This coin shows the Founder of the State of Ghana, Kwame Nkrumah.

WEST AFRICAN MONETARY UNION
When the former French West African colonies achieved statehood in 1958, they joined together to issue a common currency that included this 100-franc note.

BANQUE CENTRALE DES ÉTATS DE L'AFRIQUE DE L'OUEST
100 · 21871 · 693121871 · G.278 · 100
LE PRÉSIDENT · LE DIRECTEUR GÉNÉRAL · G.278 · 21871
CENT FRANCS

PHARAOH'S GOLD

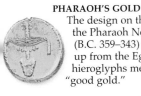

The design on this coin of the Pharaoh Nectanebo II (B.C. 359–343) is made up from the Egyptian hieroglyphs meaning "good gold."

GREEK EGYPT

Alexander the Great established Greek rule in Egypt in B.C. 332. He is portrayed on this coin, made in about B.C. 310 by his successor in Egypt, Ptolemy I.

ROMAN EGYPT

After the death of Cleopatra, the Egyptian queen, the Romans ruled Egypt and issued their own coins there. This copper coin was issued by the emperor Nero (A.D. 54–68).

THALERS IN AFRICA

Before World War II, Ethiopian currency was based on imported Austrian silver thalers (p. 32). This note, issued during the reign of Emperor Haile Selassie, is denominated as two thalers in French and Ethiopian.

SWAHILI COIN

This copper coin was issued by the Swahili Sultan of Kilwa in Tanzania during the 15th century.

SUDANESE RING MONEY

This gold ring was used to make payments in Sudan during the late 19th century.

French Madagascar: cut fragments of silver five-franc coin, about 1890

FATHER OF THE NATION

Many commemorative coins have been issued in African states to mark their independence. This 1966 gold coin portrays Jomo Kenyatta, "Father" of the Kenyan Nation.

Portuguese Mozambique: gold 2.5 maticaes, 1851

Part of the design from a French Central African banknote

British Mombasa: rupee of the Imperial British East Africa Company (Kenya), 1888

French Madagascar: 10-centimes stamp money, 1916

German East Africa (Tanzania): gold 15-rupees, 1916

South

UNITED NATIONS COIN

This Zambian 50-ngwee coin was issued in 1969 to promote the work of the United Nations Food and Agriculture Organization. The design is an ear of corn, the staple food of Zambia.

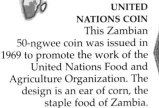

5 cents   2 cents

COINS OF NEW SOUTH AFRICA

During apartheid, South African coins had designs referring to Dutch settlers and were inscribed in Afrikaans or English. Now, they show the national arms of South Africa and local animals and plants and are inscribed in African languages, such as Xhosa and Zulu.

COLONIAL CURRENCIES

France, Germany, Britain, Italy, and Portugal all issued coins and notes for their East African colonies. They did not always introduce their own form of money, but matched the issues to those in use locally. Indian coins were widely used, so in 1888, the British issued a Mombasa rupee for use in Kenya. Rupees were also issued by the Germans in Tanganyika (now part of Tanzania), and by the Italians in Somalia. In Madagascar, the French introduced their own silver coins during the 19th century, but these were cut up by the local people, and the bits were valued in payments according to their weight.

Looking after money

MISERS HAVE NEVER been well thought of, but no one these days would question the wisdom of looking after money. Government saving schemes, such as social security and treasury bonds, and various kinds of bank accounts offer us the means of putting our money away for a "rainy day." Before the existence of savings banks, you could leave large sums of money with a merchant or a goldsmith, but the only easy way of keeping your money safe was by hiding or burying it. It was this practice of hoarding money that created the image of the miser. At home, we often use a "piggy bank" to keep our savings safe.

BURIED TREASURE
This hoard of 17th-century Persian silver coins, hidden in a small, blue-glazed pot, was discovered in 1960.

PLASTIC "PURSES"
Keeping loose change in your pocket can be a nuisance. These two gadgets, each designed to hold British one-pound coins, keep money in place.

LEATHER PURSE
This purse and the gold and silver coins it contains were left at a British court in the early 18th century. The money was saved over a long period of time: some of the coins were more than 150 years old.

Most people these days keep their savings in a bank

Ring for closing the purse

Opening for coins

English oak tree emblem appeared on the back of British pound coins during 1987

Slot for coins

METAL MONEY BOX
Lose the key to this small metal safe and you will never get your money out! The coins go into a self-sealing slot, and the notes into a curved slot on the other end. Serious savers would resist the temptation to spend their savings by leaving the key at the bank. In this way, they could only empty it into their bank savings account.

DRESS PURSE
The 19th-century dress purse above was designed to be carried on a belt, as you can see in this picture. Coins in each end would keep the purse balanced. The opening for the purse was a slit in the middle that was closed by moving the rings toward each end. However, these purses were not pick-pocket proof!

EAGLE AND CHICKS MONEY BOX
Novelty money boxes were very popular in 19th century America. This example is operated by placing a coin in the eagle's beak. A handle pushes the eagle forward to "feed" its chicks, and the coin falls into a slot at their feet.

Handle to push eagle forward

Coins were put in and taken out here

Mid-19th century British pottery piggy bank

MONEY-PIG
The most popular form for money boxes is a piggy bank, but the reason for this preference is not known. In Europe, the earliest examples are 17th-century German piggy banks, but earlier examples have been reported dating from 14th century Indonesia. The piggy banks often have to be broken in order to get the money out.

SOCK PURSE
This woven cotton sock-shaped purse from South America was also made to be worn on a belt. The long end was tucked into the belt and then pulled up to close the hole. When its wearer wanted to take coins out, he pulled it down far enough to open the hole.

TAMMANY BANK
This American novelty money box, made in 1873, has a political message. The seated figure is William "Boss" Tweed, a corrupt American politician who had his headquarters in Tammany Hall, New York. Every time you put a coin in his hand he drops it straight into his pocket!

William "Boss" Tweed sold political favors and defrauded New York City of at least $30 million

Checks and plastic

ALTHOUGH WE NORMALLY THINK OF MONEY as the coins and bills in our pockets, most of today's money cannot be put in a pocket, or even be touched, because it exists only as electronic data held in bank and business computers. Some will be changed into cash before it is used, but most of it will be paid out into another computer. Before computers were invented, money was held in written records, and payments were made by written instructions, usually on printed forms called checks. However, during the last few decades, plastic cards, some with built-in "computers," have begun to replace them.

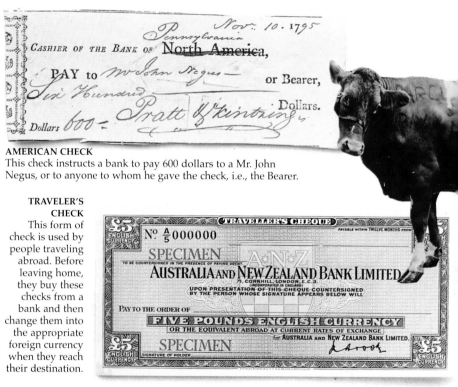

AMERICAN CHECK
This check instructs a bank to pay 600 dollars to a Mr. John Negus, or to anyone to whom he gave the check, i.e., the Bearer.

TRAVELER'S CHECK
This form of check is used by people traveling abroad. Before leaving home, they buy these checks from a bank and then change them into the appropriate foreign currency when they reach their destination.

CHINESE BILL OF EXCHANGE
500 ounces of silver had to be paid out on the order of this bill issued in 1928 by the Yi-qing-xiang Bank of Hankou, Central China.

MONEY ORDER
A French candy store used this money order to pay a supplier 13 francs, 20 centimes for goods received. The stamp in the corner shows that the five-centimes tax on money orders has been paid.

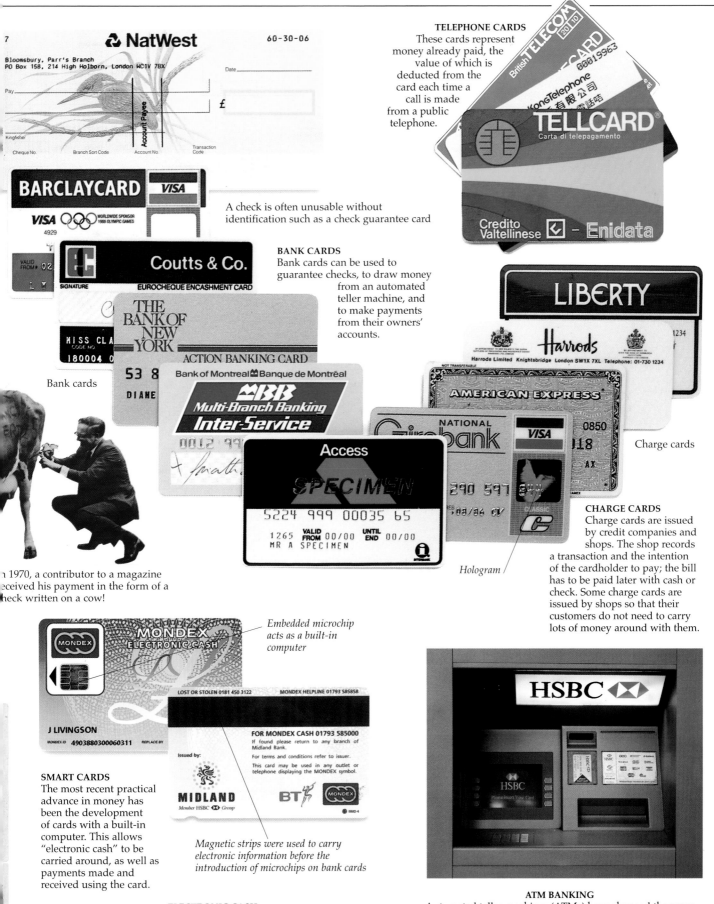

NatWest

60-30-06

Bloomsbury, Parr's Branch
PO Box 158, 214 High Holborn, London WC1V 7BX

Date :

Pay

Account Payee

£

Kingfisher

Cheque No.   Branch Sort Code   Account No.   Transaction Code

BARCLAYCARD VISA

VISA OO WORLDWIDE SPONSOR 1998 OLYMPIC GAMES

4929

VALID FROM 02

Coutts & Co.
SIGNATURE   EUROCHEQUE ENCASHMENT CARD

MISS CLA
CODE NO
180004 0

Bank cards

THE BANK OF NEW YORK

ACTION BANKING CARD

53 8

Bank of Montreal Banque de Montréal

DIANE

BB Multi-Branch Banking Inter-Service

0012 99

A check is often unusable without identification such as a check guarantee card

BANK CARDS
Bank cards can be used to guarantee checks, to draw money from an automated teller machine, and to make payments from their owners' accounts.

TELEPHONE CARDS
These cards represent money already paid, the value of which is deducted from the card each time a call is made from a public telephone.

British TELECOM 201 10
CARD 00019963
KongTelephone 有限公司
電話店

TELLCARD®
Carta di telepagamento

Credito Valtellinese ✓ - Enidata

LIBERTY

Harrods
Harrods Limited Knightsbridge London SW1X 7XL Telephone: 01-730 1234

1234

NOT TRANSFERABLE

AMERICAN EXPRESS

NATIONAL
bank
VISA
0850
18
AX

290 597
08/86 CV

CLASSIC C

Hologram

Access
SPECIMEN

5224 999 00035 65

1265 VALID FROM 00/00 UNTIL END 00/00
MR A SPECIMEN

Charge cards

CHARGE CARDS
Charge cards are issued by credit companies and shops. The shop records a transaction and the intention of the cardholder to pay; the bill has to be paid later with cash or check. Some charge cards are issued by shops so that their customers do not need to carry lots of money around with them.

In 1970, a contributor to a magazine received his payment in the form of a check written on a cow!

Embedded microchip acts as a built-in computer

MONDEX
ELECTRONIC CASH

J LIVINGSON
MONDEX ID 4903880300060311   REPLACE BY

LOST OR STOLEN 0181 450 3122   MONDEX HELPLINE 01793 585858

FOR MONDEX CASH 01793 585000
If found please return to any branch of Midland Bank.
For terms and conditions refer to issuer.
This card may be used in any outlet or telephone displaying the MONDEX symbol.

Issued by:

MIDLAND
Member HSBC Group

BT   MONDEX

SMART CARDS
The most recent practical advance in money has been the development of cards with a built-in computer. This allows "electronic cash" to be carried around, as well as payments made and received using the card.

Magnetic strips were used to carry electronic information before the introduction of microchips on bank cards

HSBC

HSBC

ATM BANKING
Automated teller machines (ATMs) have changed the ways that people use their local bank. The ATM is a bank counter that is always open, providing bank customers with all the services they normally require, through a computer interface. Customers can use a variety of cards and communicate with the machine in a range of languages.

ELECTRONIC CASH
The development of computers and the introduction of the Internet has revolutionized the use of money. Much of the money in the world now only exists as electronic records, and huge amounts of money can be passed around the world through computer links such as the Internet.

Collecting coins

THE DESIGNS AND INSCRIPTIONS on coins provide a fascinating view of the world's history. They reveal many things about the emperors, kings, and queens who issued them, as well as the traders and ordinary people who used them. Anyone can make their own collection, and one of the most interesting ways is by theme; collections featuring horses, boats, trees, and birds are shown here. The gold coins are all old and very expensive, but the coins in the plastic tray are all easy to obtain and relatively inexpensive.

SAVED FOR POSTERITY
Many of the coins now owned by collectors were once buried for safety. Luckily for the collectors, their owners were unable, or forgot, to recover them.

A soft toothbrush will not damage your coins

Rubbing alcohol

RUBBING ALCOHOL
The best way to clean coins is to wipe them with cotton balls dipped in rubbing alcohol (ask an adult to help you).

Cotton balls

PAPER ENVELOPE
Because paper envelopes d
not contain any acid, whic
causes corrosion, they will n
damage your coins. Anothe
advantage is that you ca
make notes o
the front o
then

A toothpick will get most bits of dirt off without scratching, and a pen cap is good for getting coins out of the tray

LOOKING AFTER YOUR COINS
Because old coins have been handled by lots of people, and perhaps even spent time buried in the ground, they are often very dirty. Clean them with rubbing alcohol, soap, or detergent first, and dry them thoroughly. If the dirt is stubborn, use a soft toothbrush or a piece of soft wood. If that does not work, seek advice from an experienced coin collector. The important thing is to experiment with cleaning coins that do not matter before you start on your star specimens!

A metal point can be used with caution

A magnifying glass is essential for looking at the fine details of coin designs

Sticky fingers have made this coin dirty

What not to do!

Keeping your coins clean and safely stored will make them nicer to look at and safe from corrosion. There are several things you should never do to your coins. Never use metal polish or a wire brush to clean coins – you will clean the designs right off them! Never store your coins in plastic envelopes; they may look nice when they are new, but after a while they get sticky and will ruin your coins. Never put your sticky fingers anywhere near coins, as this makes them dirty.

Never use plastic envelopes; they get sticky and may cause corrosion

A plastic envelope caused the green corrosion on this coin

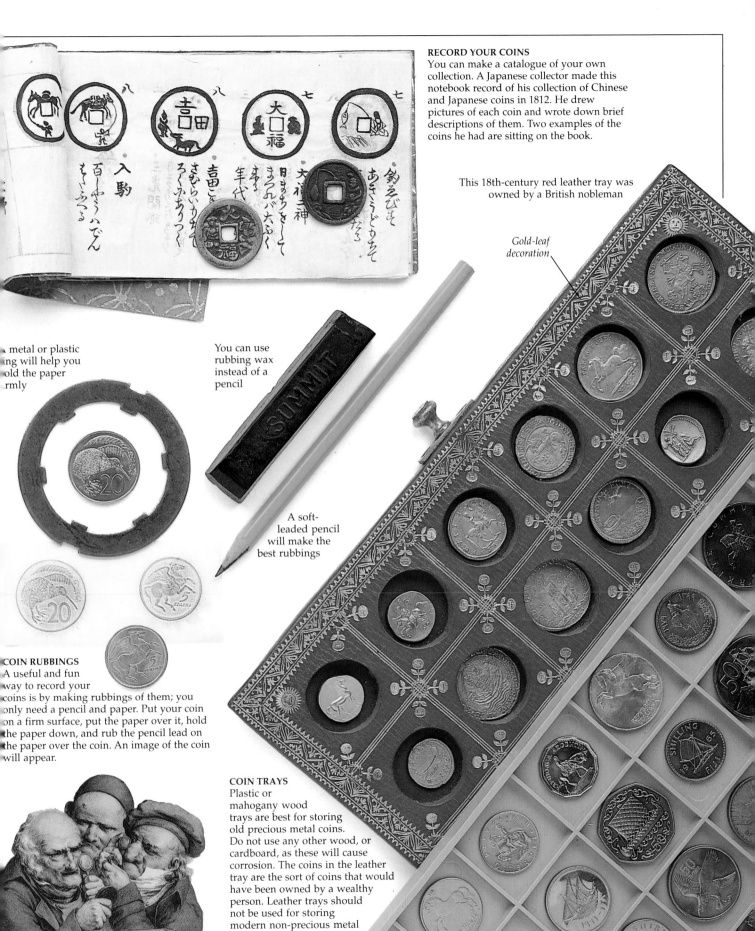

RECORD YOUR COINS

You can make a catalogue of your own collection. A Japanese collector made this notebook record of his collection of Chinese and Japanese coins in 1812. He drew pictures of each coin and wrote down brief descriptions of them. Two examples of the coins he had are sitting on the book.

This 18th-century red leather tray was owned by a British nobleman

Gold-leaf decoration

A metal or plastic ring will help you hold the paper firmly

You can use rubbing wax instead of a pencil

A soft-leaded pencil will make the best rubbings

COIN RUBBINGS

A useful and fun way to record your coins is by making rubbings of them; you only need a pencil and paper. Put your coin on a firm surface, put the paper over it, hold the paper down, and rub the pencil lead on the paper over the coin. An image of the coin will appear.

COIN TRAYS

Plastic or mahogany wood trays are best for storing old precious metal coins. Do not use any other wood, or cardboard, as these will cause corrosion. The coins in the leather tray are the sort of coins that would have been owned by a wealthy person. Leather trays should not be used for storing modern non-precious metal coins, since the leather causes these to corrode. The coins in the plastic tray are more recent, and not very expensive.

Studying coin details can be absorbing!

Did you know?

AMAZING FACTS

Counterfeiting was around long before paper money was printed. In colonial America, for example, deep purple wampum beads made of quahog clam shells were twice as valuable as white beads made from whelk shells. Some unscrupulous people painted white beads deep purple, to pass them off as purple wampum.

Quahog clam shell

One of the first coins to be minted in the United States was the 1792 half disme. (Pronounced "deem," the word was later changed to "dime.") A total of 1,500 half dismes were produced by official mint personnel, before an actual mint building was built. The coins were made in the cellar of a building at Sixth and Cherry Streets in Washington, D.C., and legend has it that some may have been coined from silverware provided by Martha Washington.

George Washington did not appear on the first U.S. coins, which portrayed icons such as Lady Liberty and the bald eagle. He rejected designs featuring his portrait because he felt it was something a king would do, not a president. His image did not appear on a coin until the 1899 commemorative "Lafayette Dollar," which featured portraits of both Washington and the Marquis de Lafayette. In 1932, his face was first featured on the quarter.

Metal money was originally exchanged in lumps or bars. A bigger lump was worth more than a smaller lump, and every time a transaction took place, the lump had to be carefully weighed to determine the value. The word "spend" comes from the Latin word, *expendere*, meaning to weigh out.

In the days before coins were made by machines, some people shaved off their edges to obtain precious metal, an act known as clipping. A pile of clippings could be melted down and sold. There were harsh punishments for clipping: A 17th-century English coin carried the message that clipping was punishable by death. To stop this practice, ridges were put around the edges of coins.

Gold is not the only treasure stashed away at the U.S. Bullion Depository at Fort Knox, Kentucky. During World War II, the original copies of the Declaration of Independence, the Constitution, the Gettysburg Address, and the Bill of Rights were secretly stored there to protect them from any possible danger. Other governments have used Fort Knox as a secure hiding place; the British Magna Carta and Crown Jewels, as well as the crown, sword, scepter, orb, and cape of St. Stephen, King of Hungary, were stored there at various times.

The crown, scepter, and sword of the Hungarian king

The Buffalo Nickel, circulated in America between 1913–1938, features an image of a majestic animal, ready to roam the wide open spaces. But the model for the coin, a buffalo named Black Diamond, never roamed outside of his home: the Central Park Zoo in New York City.

Buffalo Nickel

In 1988, Australia became the first nation to circulate plastic currency. Produced with a durable polymer material, plastic money lasts four times longer than paper money, prevents the spread of bacteria, and is virtually impossible to tear by hand. It is, however, more expensive to make. Since that time, more than 20 countries have switched to plastics: Mexico is the first nation in the Americas to issue plastic bills.

The name for a piggy bank comes from *pygg*, a type of clay used in Middle Ages to make pots for money and other things. The idea to make banks in the shape of pigs probably came from the similarity of the words.

The "life expectancy" of a coin in circulation is 30 years. The life of a paper bill depends on its denomination. A bill with a small denomination changes hands so often that it needs to be replaced in under two years, while a bill with a large denomination can last for nearly ten years.

The French word for a wedge is *coigne*. Because the dies used to stamp metal into coins were wedge-shaped, metal money was eventually given the name *coin*.

The U.S. Mint produces between 11 and 20 billion coins a year. Mint marks (a tiny letter to the right of the subject's face on the front of each coin) tell you where the coins came from: P for Philadelphia, or D for Denver.

The Federal Reserve Bank in New York City has the world's largest accumulation of gold: 269 million troy ounces (a troy ounce weighs slightly more than a standard ounce), buried five floors beneath the city streets. The bank began receiving the gold during the World Wars, when foreign countries wanted to get their gold out of Europe. Only two percent of the gold belongs to the United States. Among the 63 "account holders" at this very exclusive bank are 49 countries, and the rest are leading international organizations.

Bank is white ceramic with blue flowers.

Piggy bank

Q How much money is in circulation in the United States?

A According to the Federal Reserve, as of July 2004 there are $730 billion in U.S. coins and bills in circulation. This amount has risen rapidly in recent years, due to increasing demand from abroad. The Federal Reserve estimates that the majority of this money is held outside the U.S.

Q How does new currency enter circulation?

A While most people cash a check or go to an ATM machine to withdraw cash, American banks are supplied with cash from one of the 12 regional Federal Reserve Banks. Most medium- and large-sized banks have reserve accounts with the Fed. They pay for the cash they get by having money deducted from those accounts. Smaller banks without Fed accounts have to "buy" currency from the larger banks, who charge a fee for the service. Most countries have central banks that operate in the same way.

Q How many currencies are there in the world?

A Most countries have their own currencies, but not all. For example, some island nations in the Caribbean such as Santa Lucia and Dominica share a currency, as do a number of African nations. There are 178 different currencies in use today. A currency is considered to be in use is if it is traded on the exchange market.

Traders on the foreign exchange floor

Q What are some of the ways that paper bills are protected from counterfeiting?

A A number of security features prevent paper money from being reproduced easily. Many bills include watermarks, faint images, similar to the larger pictures, that are only visible when the bill is held up to the light. Plastic security threads may also be embedded in the paper. These glow when held under an ultraviolet light. Color-shifting inks, whose color looks different at different angles, are sometimes used, and the bill may also be printed all over with tiny words (called microprinting) that are difficult to duplicate. Adding holograms or kinograms (images wich change when tilted) to currency is the latest trend in anti-counterfeiting, but printers are always searching for new ways to stay ahead of the counterfeiting curve.

Q What happens to worn-out paper money?

A When banks have an excess of cash on hand, they deposit it with the Federal Reserve Bank. The Fed checks the condition of the individual notes to determine if they are fit to circulate again. About a third of the notes are not; these are destroyed by shredding. Some of the shredded bills are recycled into products such as insulation and stationery. Visitors to the Fed also may receive a small bag of shredded cash as a souvenir. Any counterfeit bills are separated and sent to the United States Secret Service for investigation. When the Federal Reserve needs new money, it orders it from the Bureau of Engraving and Printing.

Q What is the foreign exchange market?

A The value of one currency compared to another is called the exchange rate. The rate is determined at the foreign exchange markets of cities like New York, London, Tokyo, and Paris, where dealers buy and sell currency of different countries. The rate fluctuates every minute of every day, depending on supply and demand. In basic terms, if Americans want to buy British goods, they need British money, or pounds, to pay for them. The demand for the pound goes up, so its value goes up. If British goods are too costly, the demand for them goes down and the value of the pound falls.

Holograms used to combat counterfeiting

Q How is money exchanged on the Internet today?

A As the Internet has taken its place as an important part of people's lives, it has also emerged as a new way of exchanging money. While most online purchases are still made with credit cards, a number of clearing houses have been set up to give anyone with an e-mail address the ability to send and receive payments in a number of global currencies.

Record Breakers

LARGEST GOLD COIN:
A 68-pound (31-kg) coin issued in Austria in 2004, with a face value of 100,000 Euros. The coin features a replica of the Vienna Philharmonic Orchestra's hall, giving it its nickname, Big Phil. Fifteen of the 24-carat gold disks were made by the Austrian mint.

MOST VALUABLE COIN:
A 1933 Double Eagle gold piece sold for close to $8 million dollars at an auction. All the other Double Eagles in circulation (except for two sent to the Smithsonian, right) were destroyed in 1933 when the U.S. went off the gold standard.

WORLD'S LARGEST BANKNOTE:
In 1998, to mark the Centennial of Philippine independence from Spanish rule, the government issued a giant banknote, measuring 8½ by 14 inches (the size of American legal paper). A thousand of the notes were printed.

WORLD'S SMALLEST BANKNOTE:
A note issued in Romania in 1917 measured 34 mm by 45 mm—about the size of a postage stamp.

Timeline of banking

T HE STORY OF MONEY is also told through the way most people store money: banking. A bank is a financial institution where people keep their money safe. Banks also extend credit to their customers. The word "bank" is derived from the Italian word for bench, *banca*. Money lenders in Italy made transactions with their customers in the town center, each lender operating from his own park bench. Here is a timeline of banking history.

European knights on crusade

c. 3000 BCE

The origins of banking in Mesopotamia, as temples and palaces are used to provide safe storage for "deposits" of grain and other valuables. Eventually, private houses were also set up for the same purpose.

c. 1792–1750 BCE

Under the reign of Hammurabi, King of Babylon, a set of laws known as the Code of Hammurabi is issued. The Code includes laws that govern banking.

c. 600 BCE

The first surviving mention of a merchant banker in the ancient world. The banker, named Pythius, trades throughout Asia Minor.

c. 394 BCE

A slave in Athens named Pasion becomes the wealthiest banker in the city. He gains citizenship (and freedom) because he gives generous amounts of money to the state.

King Hammurabi

390 BCE

The Gauls launch a surprise attack on the Capitoline Hill in Rome, where the city's reserves of money are kept. Squawking geese alert Roman soldiers, and the invasion is foiled. The Romans build a shrine on the hill to Moneta, the goddess of warning; from her name we get the words for money and mint.

323 BCE

State granaries function as banks in Egypt. Payments are made by transfer from one "account" to another without any money changing hands.

c. CE 900

The Chinese government issues paper money. Its use is widespread for the next 500 years, until the Mongol conquest.

1095–1270

The Europeans launch Crusades to reclaim the Holy Lands of the Middle East. The need to transfer large sums of money for troops and supplies provides a boost to the emergence of European banking.

1171

The Bank of Venice is founded in Italy, in order to loan money to the government.

1400s–1600s

The Medici family, based in Florence, Italy, become leading figures during the Renaissance era. Their wealth was first acquired largely through banking.

1401

The Bank of Barcelona is founded in Barcelona, Italy. This bank is considered to be the first to offer the basic banking operations we are familiar with today. For example, the bank held deposits, exchanged currency, and lent money.

1450s

The Fuggers, a German banking family, reach their height. They dominate banking in Europe, but when the royal houses of France and Spain default on their loans, the bank goes under.

1545

Britain's King Henry VIII legalizes interest rates on loans but sets an upper limit of ten percent per year. His legislation is annulled by Parliament under the rule of Edward VI in 1552.

1566

The Royal Exchange is founded in England, to enable London to compete as a financial power.

1609

The Bank of Amsterdam is founded in Holland. It was chartered to receive deposits of gold and silver.

1619

Hamburg Girobank is founded in Germany. It is Germany's first commercial bank, and lasts until its takeover by the state-run Reichsbank in 1875.

1630s

British goldsmiths, who sometimes deal in coins and let customers use their safes for depositing gold and other valuables, begin to evolve into bankers.

1659

A British check is issued for 400 pounds sterling. It is the oldest existing check.

1668

Sveriges Riksbank (the Bank of Sweden) is founded in Stockholm. It is the world's first central bank.

1660

During a shortage of silver coins, the Stockholm Bank of Sweden issues Europe's first printed paper money.

1694

The Banks of England and Scotland are founded to serve the English and Scottish governments.

1716

The first public bank in France, the Banque Generale, opens its doors to customers.

1728

The Royal Bank of Scotland introduces a system in which certain people are given a line of credit against future deposits; this is the origin of the overdraft.

Catherine the Great

1768

The first banks are established in Russia. They are created by Catherine the Great to help finance Russia's war with the Ottoman Empire (present-day Turkey). The bank issued paper currency the next year.

1772

Scotland establishes eight bank branches throughout the country, making it the first country in the world to establish a nationwide system of branch banking.

1780

The Bank of Pennsylvania is founded to raise money for the Continental Army. It is the first American bank to be established since the Declaration of Independence.

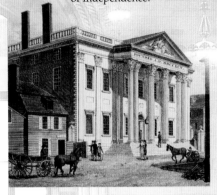

The Bank of Pennsylvania

1791

The First Bank of the United States is formed in an early attempt to centralize America's banking system. It becomes the largest corporation in the country but its charter is not renewed in 1811 because many Americans are uncomfortable with the existence of one all-powerful bank.

1803

The Louisiana Purchase (effectively doubling the size of the United States) is funded through loans to the U.S. government from two British banks, Barings and Hopes. French leader Napoleon sells the land to the U.S. for 15 million dollars.

1816

Members of the Rothschild family, a dynasty of German Jewish bankers, are made barons.

1836–1865

The U.S. enters the Free Banking Era. Almost anyone is allowed to print money— from a restaurant to a railroad company. There are as many as 8,000 different issuers of money during this era, and counterfeits are almost impossible to detect.

1864

With Abraham Lincoln's support, the National Bank Act in the United States puts an end to the Free Banking Era by providing a national currency.

1865

The Latin Monetary Union is established in France, with members including Belgium, Italy, Switzerland, and Greece. Members kept their own currency name and coin design, but they all used a common standard of currency.

1881

Postal orders (money orders purchased at the post office) are introduced in Britain.

1914

The U.S. Federal Reserve system is established with 12 regional banks.

OCTOBER 24, 1929

Black Thursday: the Great Crash of the New York Stock Exchange

1929–33

The Great Depression. The failure of banks is widespread, and the remaining banks cut back on lending, so many people and businesses go bankrupt.

1933

The FDIC (Federal Deposit Insurance Corporation) is created in the United States to insure bank deposits.

1950

The first American drive-through banking window opens in Columbus, Ohio.

1969

The International Monetary Fund (IMF) creates the Special Drawing Rate; participating countries can draw funds from reserves in times of crisis.

1972

A patent for the automatic teller machine is issued to Don Wetzel.

1978

SMART cards, patented in 1974 by Roland Moreno, the inventor of the microchip, are mass produced for the first time.

1979

The European Monetary System is created to link the currencies of the European Union.

Newspaper announcing the great stock-market crash of October 24, 1929

1988

The savings-and-loan crisis peaks in the U.S. Hundreds of savings-and-loan associations go under, costing the federal fund that insures them billions of dollars.

1990

The four biggest banks in the world are all Japanese. In 1970, the top ten banks were all American.

1999

The euro is introduced into the countries belonging to the European Union. By 2002, euro banknotes and coins replace the former national currencies in member states.

2005

A major survey shows that banking is the fastest growing Internet activity.

Representatives of the U.S. and France exchange documents in the Louisiana Purchase

Find out more

IF YOU WANT TO FIND OUT MORE ABOUT money, there is a wealth of opportunities for you. Pay a visit to the places where paper notes are printed and coins are created. Touring these facilities not only reveals the history of money, but may also give you a chance to see millions of dollars in new cash on the production line. If you live near a city with a central or Federal Reserve bank, check for tour information on the Internet. A number of Fed branches in the United States feature excellent historical museums, as well as free on-site tours to explain the practice of central banking. You might also be able to schedule a behind-the-scenes tour of your local bank. If you don't already have one, consider opening a savings account while you are there. A visit to a stock exchange will give you a glimpse of the action on the trading floor. If you think you might be interested in starting a coin collection, look in your local newspaper or online for information about local coin shows or coin-collecting clubs.

VISIT A MONEY MUSEUM
Many museums have collections of coins and paper money, allowing visitors to view rare and ancient forms of currency that they would otherwise only get to read about—such as these two beautiful decadrachms from the ancient Greek colony of Syracuse.

START A COIN COLLECTION
Starting your own coin or paper money collection can be a great hobby. The recent issue of state quarters in the United States has encouraged many people to start collections. There are plenty of books, Web sites, and magazines devoted to collecting. You could also look for a rare-coin dealer in your area, and ask his or her advice on the best way to get started.

USEFUL WEB SITES

www.money.org
Explore the world of money on the home page of the American Numismatic Association.

www.usmint.gov/kids/
The Internet home of the U.S. mint tells you about the history you have in your pockets.

www.moneyfactory.com/kids/start.html
A fun interactive site for kids from the Bureau of Engraving and Printing.

www.fdic.gov/about/learn/learning/
A kid's guide to the FDIC and banking

www.federalreserveeducation.org/fed101/
An interactive guide to the Federal Reserve system reveals the life of a check or dollar bill

A TON OF GOLD BRICKS
Tour the vault of the Federal Reserve Bank in New York City and you will see one-third of all the monetary gold in the world. There is enough gold here to cover a a football field. It is kept in special "cages," one for each nation's central bank. When one country sells gold to another, it is moved between the cages by workers wearing shoe covers to protect their feet from dropped bricks.

ATTEND A COIN SHOW
Coin shows, where dealers show and sell their collections, are frequently scheduled on weekends across the country. Check the newspaper or the Internet for a show near you. You'll be able to chat with dealers and see some amazing coins.

OPEN A SAVINGS ACCOUNT
An important part of learning about money is finding out how to hang onto it. Setting up your own savings account will let you take the first steps into the world of financial responsibility. Many banks offer free savings accounts for children under a specified age. Most banks will accept a low deposit to open a kid's account, and you will earn interest on the money you save.

Minting of a 2004 nickel marking the Louisiana Purchase

This is the die from which the special nickels are stamped.

The Royal Canadian Mint, Ottawa, Ontario

This tool rotates as it polishes each coin.

WHERE MONEY COMES FROM
Before the bills and change got in your pocket, they were printed or minted. Check the Internet and find out where your currency is made. In the United States, for example, paper money is printed at the Federal Bureau of Engraving and Printing in Washington, D.C., and coins are made in one of the two branches of the U.S. Mint, in Denver or Philadelphia. Most of these facilities offer informative tours.

Places to Visit

UNITED STATES MINT
PHILADELPHIA, PA AND DENVER, CO
Tours cover the history of the Mint as well as all stages of the minting process, from creating the original design to striking the coins.

BUREAU OF ENGRAVING AND PRINTING, WASHINGTON, D.C.
WESTERN CURRENCY FACILITY, FORT WORTH, TX
Watch millions of dollars being printed right before your eyes at these two facilities, and learn all about the production of currency.

MUSEUM OF AMERICAN FINANCIAL HISTORY, NEW YORK, NY
This museum explores significant events in U.S. history from a financial perspective.

MONEY MUSEUM, COLORADO SPRINGS, COLORADO
America's largest museum dedicated to numismatics consists of over 400,000 objects.

FEDERAL RESERVE BANK OF NEW YORK, NEW YORK, NY
Feast your eyes on a small portion of the world's largest cache of gold.

FEDERAL RESERVE BANK OF CLEVELAND, CLEVELAND, OH
Take a first-hand look at the Fed's cash processing operation on this tour.

FEDERAL RESERVE BANK OF CHICAGO, CHICAGO, IL
See what a million dollars looks like, and try your skill at detecting actual counterfeit bills.

NATIONAL NUMISMATIC COLLECTION, SMITHSONIAN INSTITUTION, WASHINGTON, D.C.
This is one of the most important collections in the world, with 1.6 million objects.

FEDERAL RESERVE BANK OF RICHMOND, RICHMOND, VA
The Money Museum tells the story of money with a focus on Colonial America.

FEDERAL RESERVE BANK OF ATLANTA, ATLANTA, GA
The Visitor's Center and Monetary Museum takes you from bartering to the present day.

Glossary

ALLOY A mixture containing two or more elements, at least one of which is metallic, fused together. Brass, for example, is an alloy of zinc and copper.

ASSIGNATS Treasury notes issued during the French Revolution to redeem the huge public debt. The paper currency was made legal tender in 1798, but the value of the currency fell so much it did not even cover printing costs.

French assignat, 1793

BANKNOTE A bill or piece of paper money, especially one issued by a nation's central bank. Banknotes are usually printed on paper or plastic.

BARTER A trade in which goods or services are exchanged directly for other goods and services, without the use of money. Barter is the oldest form of trade and remains an important means of trade for countries using currencies that are not readily convertible on world currency exchange markets.

BILL OF EXCHANGE An unconditional payment demand for a specific sum of money, payable either at once or at a specified future date. A bill of exchange is drawn up by the seller and presented to the buyer. Sometimes called "drafts," bills of exchange are the most commonly used instrument in international trade.

BLANKS A featureless, coin-shaped circle of metal onto which a coin's design is minted, or marked.

BULLION Bars or ingots of precious metals, usually cast in standardized sizes

CACAO BEAN A bean that grows inside large pods on the cacao tree. Cacao beans are used to make cocoa and chocolate, and were used as currency in Pre-Columbian Mexico.

CARAT A measure of the purity of gold. Pure gold is 24 carats.

CIRCULATION The spread or transmission of money to a wider group or area. In the United States, money enters into circulation through distribution from the central Federal Reserve Banks to individual banks, and then to consumers.

COIN CLIPPING The practice of trimming small shavings from the edges of coins made from pure metals, and melting them down for sale. The clipping was so minimal that the coins could still be used as currency.

COLOR PROOF In banknote production, a representation of the final printed product, used to check color accuracy and other printing elements.

COMMEMORATIVE COINS A special coin featuring a design honoring a particular person, place, or historical event.

Cowrie shells

COMMODITY Any raw material, such as oil, wheat, silver, soybeans, or livestock. Commodities can be sold on the spot, or on a commodities exchange, where people invest in a contract to buy or sell goods by a specified future date. When people buy commodities, they hope the price will rise, so they can sell at a profit.

COWRIE Any of many tropical marine gastropods with highly polished, usually colorful shells, which are used as currency in India, Africa, and Thailand.

Holder for cowrie shells

CUNEIFORM A system of writing used in the ancient Near East, perhaps the earliest known writing system. Cuneiform writers used small, wedge-shaped tools to make characters on wet clay tablets, which were later fired to harden and preserve them.

CUPRO-NICKEL An alloy of approximately 75 percent copper and 25 percent nickel, widely used all over the world for coinage because of its long-wearing properties and low production cost.

CURRENCY A country's official unit of monetary exchange; the metal or paper money issued by the government as legal tender.

DENOMINATION The face value of a coin or banknote in the currency of the issuing country. The denomination is usually stamped or printed on the coin or banknote itself.

DIE A device that is used for shaping metal; for example, in minting coins

DISME The original spelling of "dime," or one-tenth of a dollar. This term was in widespread use in the 17th century.

DOUBLOON An early Spanish gold coin. Because only very wealthy people used doubloons, they did not usually wear out. In addition, gold does not corrode like silver, so there are some beautiful examples of these coins still in existence.

Minting die

DRACHMA A silver coin used in ancient Greece, about the same size as an American dime, but thicker.

DUCAT A gold coin once in use in several European countries

ELECTRUM A naturally occurring alloy of silver and gold. Electrum was used to make some of the first coins in the world.

EURO A common currency that has replaced the individual currencies of most (but not all) of the countries that are members of the European Union

EXPORT Any goods or services that are sold abroad. Export can also describe the actual shipment or transfer of these goods and services out of a country.

FLORIN A unit of currency formerly used in the Netherlands and other parts of Europe

FORGERY The process of making or changing objects or documents with the intention to deceive someone. Fraud is the use of objects obtained through forgery.

FORT KNOX The site of the U.S. Bullion Depository in Kentucky. The gold vaults in Fort Knox opened in 1937.

GOLD DUST The particles and flakes (and sometimes tiny nuggets) of gold obtained by mining

GREENBACKS A nickname for American dollars, originally used to describe the banknotes issued by the U.S. government during the Civil War. They were given the name because the backs of the notes were printed in green ink.

HIEROGLYPHICS A system of writing in which the characters consist of pictures of actual objects, animals, or human beings, instead of letters and words

Holey dollar, with dump

HOLEY DOLLAR A coin with a hole in the center, the official currency of New South Wales, Australia, from 1813 to 1822. The circle cut from the center, called a "dump," was also official currency.

INGOT A mass of metal, such as gold, cast in a mold to give it a convenient shape (usually a block or bar) for storage or transportation. Ingots are later re-melted so the metal can be cast or rolled.

INTAGLIO A type of printmaking in which an image is etched onto a metal plate. Ink is then applied to the etched areas beneath the plate's surface. When pressed against damp paper, the inked plate prints the image in reverse.

LETTERPRESS a printing method that stamps ink onto paper from a raised surface. Also called block printing.

LITHOGRAPHY A printing process that is based on the fact that water and oil will not mix together.

MANILLA A copper ring used as currency in West Africa from the 15th to the 20th centuries

MINT The official government building where coins are struck, or minted

MINTING The process of forming coins by stamping, punching, or printing. The basic process of minting—stamping a design onto metal by pressing it between two hard metal dies—was invented around 2,600 years ago in Lydia (present-day Turkey).

MISER A stingy person who hoards money and possessions and lives frugally, so that he or she can hang on to money

MONETARY UNION The result of two or more governments deciding to share a common currency. The European Economic and Monetary Union is an example.

MONEY ORDER A check that a customer can buy for a small fee from a post office or financial institution, issued to a specific payee for a specific amount

OWL COINS Silver coins issued in Ancient Greece featuring the image of an owl, considered a special bird. Greeks traded throughout the world with these coins and soon other nations issued their own coins featuring owl designs.

PESO A silver coin used in the Spanish colonies of the Americas; also, a modern form of currency in various countries

PIECE OF EIGHT An early Spanish coin with a face value of eight reales. The U.S. dollar was originally valued at the same amount as this coin.

PLATE MONEY Huge, very heavy copper coins once issued in Sweden. Many of these plate coins weighed more than 4 pounds (2 kg).

PUNCH A tool used to make holes in minting

SECURITY THREAD A metallic or polyester strip that is embedded in a banknote paper during its manufacure. Bills that contain a security thread are difficult to forge because they cannot be reproduced using a color photocopier.

Greek owl coin

Manillas were made of copper

Manillas

SCISSEL The strip of metal that is left behind after coins are stamped.

SIEGE MONEY Currency issued at various times in history when a city was cut off by a siege. This money was often used to pay for soldiers and necessities when the official currency ran out.

SMART CARD A card, about the size of a credit card, that contains a computer chip and is used to store or process information

TOKEN A metal or plastic coinlike disk that can be used as a substitute for coins to redeem a product or service, such as a ride on the subway

Marks on a touchstone

TOUCHSTONE A black stone used to test the quality (in carats) of a gold coin. A trader would rub the coin against the stone, then compare the streak left behind to a set of thin gold needles of various carats. If the streak matched the 10-carat needle, for example, the coin was known to be of 10-carat gold.

TRADE The exchange of goods and services; all the buying and selling that takes place in domestic and foreign markets

UPSETTING MILL In coin minting, a rotating wheel with a groove on its edge that creates a raised rim on both sides of the blank when it is rolled along the groove

WAMPUM Small tubelike beads made from polished white and purple clam shells and fashioned into strings or belts. Wampum was used by American Indian tribes as money and as jewelry.

WATERMARK A design that is embossed into a piece of paper during its production. The watermark can be seen when the paper is held up to the light. Watermarks are one way that banknote printers seek to prevent the counterfeiting of paper money.

Index

Acknowledgments

The publisher and the author would like to thank:

Thomas Keenes for additional design assistance; Peter Hayman, (pp. 58–59), Karl Shone (pp. 26–27), Kate Warren (pp. 8–9) for special photography; the staff of the British Museum who helped, particularly Janet Larkin, Suzie Chan, Virginia Hewitt, Andy Meadows, Sue Crundwell, Brendan Moore, and Keith Howes of the Coins and Medals Department; Travellers Exchange Corporation plc for the supply of international currencies; The Museum of Mankind; The Royal Mint; De La Rue; HSBC; European Monetary Institute; The National Westminster Bank; Pollock's Toy Museum; The National Philatelic Society; The Hungarian International Bank; G. Smith & Sons; Sothebys of London; Dr. Fergus Duncan; Coin Craft; Kiwi Fruits, London; Barclays Bank Ltd; Robert Tye; Steve Cribb; Bill Barrett; Howard Simmons; Andrew Oddy; Clare Nelson; Graham Dyer; Kevin Clancy; Edwin Green; Margaret, Laurence, Dunstan, Althea and Ruth Cribb; James Taylor; Anna and Katie Martin; Jane Parker for the index.

Picture credits:

(t=top, b=bottom, m=middle, l=left, r=right)
AKG Photo: 28m
Aldus Archive: 22bl, 37tr, 51m
Ancient Art & Architecture Collection: 6bm
The British Library: 60t
The British Museum: 7tl, 17, 40m, 46m, 60b
Burgerbibliothek, Bern: 32m
J. Allan Cash Photolibrary: 8br, 36mr, 56ml
Dennis R. Cooper: 30t
E.T. Archive: 34bl, 52m
Mary Evans Picture Library: 8tl, 22m, 24tl, 24bl, 25t, 25ml, 31r, 35ml, 36tm, 38b, 39tl, 42tl, 46b, 50, 53m, 56tr
Fotomas Index: 21tl
Robert Harding Picture Library: 29bm, 30b, 38tl
Michael Holford: 11mr, 46tl
Hulton-Deutsch: 33tr, 57b
Hutchison Library: 52tl
Mansell Collection: 13m, 40tl, 42bl
National Portrait Gallery, London: 34mr

Peter Newark's Pictures: 28tl, 48, 49
Pollock's Toy Museum, London: 56b
Popperfoto: 29mr
Punch: 58–59m
Louvre/c. Réunion des Musées Nationaux: 34tl
The Royal Mint: 14–15
Spectrum Colour Library: 41l
Worthing Museum & Art Gallery: 57mr
Zefa: 12mr, 27tr, 28bl, 42mr, 59bm

American Numismatic Association: 69tl
AP Wideworld: 65br
Bridgeman Art Library: Louvre, Paris, France 66cl; Private Collection, Archives Charmet 66tr
Corbis: 67tl; Archivo Iconografico, S.A. 66br; Craig Aurness 69tr; Bettmann 67bl; Yves Forestier 65tr; Wolfgang Kaehler 64tr; Lee Snider 68br; Joseph Sohm; ChromoSohm Inc. 64-65
DK: Chas Howson/British Museum 70tl, 71cr, 71cl; Nick Nicholls/British Museum 71bl; David Garner/Exeter Museum 71tr; Dave King/Pitt Rivers Museum 70bl; Science Museum London 70br; Yorkshire Museum 70cr

Getty Images: 67cr, 69bc; AFP 65bl
Smithsonian Museum of American History: 68tl
US Mint Image: 64cl

Jacket images: Front: Corbis: Jose Luis Pelaez, Inc. (cb). DK Images: Chas Howson/The British Museum (tc, tcl, tcr, tr). Back: DK Images: Chas Howson/The British Museum (cra, crb, tl).

Illustrators: Thomas Keenes: 10m, 20m, 54t and b, 55t and b; Kathleen McDougall: 12t, 32t; John Woodcock: 29tr

Picture Research: Kathy Lockley; Frances Vargo

The objects on the following pages are smaller than their actual size: pp. 6–7; 8–9; 12–13; 14–15; 26–27; 58–59; 60–61; 62–63. All current banknotes are reproduced at a reduced size, and in some cases in black and white, according to the reproduction regulations of the country concerned.